Beyond the Bullet

Beyond the Bullet

Personal Stories of Gun Violence Aftermath

Heidi Yewman

Photographs by Kathy Carlisle

DASH Consulting, Inc.
Vancouver, Washington

Published by DASH Consulting, Inc.
Vancouver, Washington
www.beyondthebulletbook.com

First edition
Printed in the United States of America

ISBN: 978-0-615-27738-7
Library of Congress Control Number: 2009901202

Photography by Kathy Carlisle
Editing by Linda Meyer
Cover design by Jake Carlisle
Interior design by Jennifer Omner

*This book is dedicated to the families and loved ones
of the thirty thousand people killed each year by gun violence
and to the seventy thousand who are shot each year and survive.
May you find peace.*

The process

I found the people I interviewed for this book in various ways. Some were referred to me, some called me after hearing about this project, some I approached at gun violence-prevention events, and some I contacted after reading about them in the paper. I didn't interview anyone who was less than a year into his or her journey, to allow for the perspective that often comes with the passage of time. My only requirement was that each person had been affected by gun violence. Personal views on guns and gun ownership were not the focus of these interviews; although in some cases those views did come out.

The interviews were conversational. I usually began by asking about the person who died, or in the case of being shot, *What happened?* I followed up with several prepared questions that helped jump-start the narrative. I recorded and transcribed each interview. Each chapter is the voice of the interviewee, with only light edits—for length, clarification, and understanding. I tried to preserve the interviewees' tone and cadence so that the reader could really hear their voices as they spoke. I found that when people discuss traumatic situations they don't always speak about the event in sequential order or use textbook grammar. And that's okay. These were unrehearsed conversations, not polished presentations.

The ages and references to times and dates were recorded at the time of the interview and are reflected in the introduction of each chapter. In some cases it's been several years since the interviews took place. The time span between when something happened and when it was talked about during the interview is relative to the date of the interview.

Proceeds from the sale of this book will go to the registered nonprofit
Families & Friends of Violent Crime Victims

www.fnfvcv.org

Introduction: Why I wrote this book

I wasn't in the library or the cafeteria. I didn't hear the screams or the pop of the guns. I wasn't in the building or even in the state. I was, however, profoundly affected by what happened at Columbine High School on that horrible day in April 1999. It wasn't so much that I had studied in that library or ate in that cafeteria or that most of the teachers teaching that day had taught me thirteen years earlier, it was that I couldn't fathom something so evil happening in a place that felt so safe for me.

I remember sitting at Dave Sanders' funeral, the sole teacher who was killed while saving lives during the rampage. He had coached me, taught me, and touched my life. I hadn't seen him since I graduated, and probably never would have, but his senseless death and the deaths of the other kids who walked the same halls I had walked changed me. I felt personally assaulted and it moved me to action. I sat and cried along with former teachers and classmates in a hard wooden pew of a crowded church on that rainy day, and I vowed to do everything I could to prevent this from happening again. I had no idea of the power that vow would have, and how making it would change my life.

Over the next year, I obsessed over the details of the rampage and collected as much information as I could about the families, the shooters, and the circumstances that lead to such a tragedy. What struck me most was how differently each family dealt with their loss. Some immediately sued anyone they thought could be responsible. Some became gun control advocates; some went on religious pilgrimages; some went into hiding; and some simply appeared to melt away into their anguish. What they did have in common was wanting their child's life to matter and for their life and death never to be forgotten.

That year I also learned about gun violence in America and how prevalent it is. I was surprised and insulted by the National Rifle Association's (NRA) decision to proceed with its annual convention in Denver just two weeks after the massacre. I also learned about the lax U.S. gun laws and how accessible guns are to everyone in America.

It wasn't until May 2000 that the events at Columbine and all that I had learned in the intervening year culminated in the Million Mom March in Washington, D.C. I stood on stage among other state organizers overlooking a sea of over seven hundred and fifty thousand people, many of whom wore t-shirts and held posters professing that the life of their child, sister, brother, grandchild, mother, or father *mattered*. Their shirts and posters all had a photo of their loved one along with their loved one's birthdate and the date they died from gun violence. As I walked through the crowd, an overwhelming wave of emotion hit me every time I read a t-shirt or sign. I wanted to know how they got through each day. What were the circumstances? How does it feel to wear a shirt like that? How do you make that person's life matter, and how do you deal with all the emotions that come with violent loss?

As my life turned from keep-everyone-happy stay-at-home-mom to adversarial advocate, I entered a world of meanness. I received nasty letters from NRA members informing me that I am going to hell, my kids are going to turn out gay, and that I am an uninformed idiot. From my debates and discussions with "the other side," I also learned that to many of them, seventeen- and eighteen-year-olds are not kids; that gang members killed by gun violence should not be included in statistics because they don't matter and should die anyway; and that the fifty-one percent of suicide deaths should not be included in the statistics because "those people didn't want to live anyway." I was appalled that thousands of people could be dismissed as irrelevant in a discussion as to why we should reduce gun violence. Their solution seemed to be, *Just adjust the statistics, and we really don't have a problem.* Problem is, all those eighteen-year-olds, gang members, and suicide victims have moms, dads, sisters, brothers, children, grandparents, and friends who miss them and have not been the same since their death.

What I found was that through the debates, discussions, and arguments, it always came down to statistics and how they are manipulated. Both sides use statistics to bolster their case and make their argument relevant and important. With each death a family is torn apart, and their lives are never the same. When a mother whose child was killed in 1998 looks at the 29,887 who died that year, she wishes that number were 29,886. A reduction by one does not make a big difference to the rest of us, but to her it does; it is her life and her struggle. It's not about the statistics. It's about the lives that are affected by violent loss. Until we see those lives as more than numbers, violent death "by bullet" will continue.

That is what inspired this book. If people can see more than a number and become connected at a personal level, I truly believe we can reduce the level of gun violence in our country and stop having meaningless arguments about numbers.

As I met more and more people who have lost loved ones to gun violence, I started asking them about their lives and how their loss has affected them. I sought out more in-depth stories. I looked for books on the subject and could only find books that explained why more guns make us safer, and how gun control is bad for all of us. I found these types of books insulting after meeting so many people who were just trying to get from day to day without being crushed by their overwhelming loss. I decided that their stories needed to be told and I would be the one to tell them.

Contents

Lonnie Feather — *Attempted murder* 14

John Johannessen — *Daughter shot* 20

Christie Toribara — *Son committed suicide* 28

Mary Leigh Blek — *Son murdered* 36

Robin Shanafelt — *Husband killed* 44

Liz Julee — *Mother committed suicide* 52

John Oerter — *Granddaughter murdered* 58

Bobbie Peyser — *Daughter murdered* 66

Rick Bath — *Friend murdered* 74

Michelle Jeffries — *Son murdered* 82

Jenny Wieland — *Daughter killed* 92

Cindy Johnson — *Fiancé committed suicide* 100

Sandie Williamson — *Son murdered* 108

Kari Oswold — *Husband committed suicide* 118

Tasha Ross — *Son murdered* 130

Tom Mauser — *Son murdered* 140

Loni Roberts — *Husband killed* 148

Tom Johnson (TJ) — *Teacher at Columbine High School* 156

My journey 164

Gun violence in perspective 166

Victim resources 172

About the photographer 175

Lonnie Feather

After being shot three times in the head by her boy-friend Michael, Lonnie played dead for seven hours until a SWAT team finally rescued her. She is a glass artist who continues to live and work in the same house where in 2001 at forty-one she almost lost her life. The scar on her check is still visible. She has decided not to have plastic surgery to fix it. "It is who I am now. It is my star nebula. I think my scar looks like the opening of heaven."

I was sitting on the couch. He came up to me and pinched my neck until I passed out. When I came to, I could see the gun. It was aimed at my head, and he fired. I heard the second shot but did not feel pain. My brain took over and separated from my body. My brain decided the best thing for me to do was play dead so he wouldn't shoot me again. I slumped down on the couch and went out because it would have been too horrible to remember.

He put a pillow over my head and shot two more times. It was very loud; I still have damage in my ear. When I came to, I noticed the pillow on my head, and I had one foot on the floor so I could feel the vibrations of him walking around. I knew my only chance for survival was to be smarter than he was. I figured out I was alive. I was expecting to see a white light and I thought, *If I am dead, I will see my dad, and he will come down and get me.* Then I noticed my fingers and my toes and knew that I needed to reduce my heart rate and my breathing so I would look like I was at least unconscious.

Lonnie Feather

When he went out of the room to answer the door, I reached up for the phone on the table and dialed 911. I said, "I have been shot in the head twice," gave my address, and then hung up. I didn't want to give him any reason to shoot me again, so I was hoping to lie in the exact position. For four hours, I had not moved until I reached for the phone. When the police came, it became a hostage situation. I lay there for another three hours, hoping he would commit suicide.

He was calm. He sat at the desk at the computer playing games and writing plans on what to do with my body. He was going to call my mom and tell her we were going out of town for a few days; he was going to call my work and tell them I was sick. He was going to hook up my truck on the back of his motor home. Part of the note said, "duct tape hands, feet, mouth, plastic in shop." He was deciding what to do with me. I am sure he was going to put my body in his motor home, drive off to a remote location, and bury my body.

The best thing for me to do was play dead so he wouldn't shoot me again.

I knew they [the SWAT team] could see him in the window and wondered why they couldn't just shoot him. I just wanted them to get me out. He finally decided to give himself up, took his shirt and hat off, and walked out the front door. The paramedics came in, put me on a little tiny board, and got me to the hospital where they performed an emergency tracheotomy because my throat was swelling from the wound.

That was the scariest part of everything—reading that note. It was the most horrible thing. I noticed that every time the words *duct tape* came up, it was this shock for me, so I had to deal with it. I had to transform it. For me to actually go into my work-shop and get the duct tape he would have used, to pull it off the shelf, to handle it, to tear it, to touch it would have been horrible. But I knew I had to do it. I had to turn it into something else. Otherwise, I would have been walking into the shop saying, *Oh my god! There is the duct tape.*

I did a whole series of artwork on being shot. Art helped me through this; it was a process. The last one I did, called "For all the women who have died: duct tape, hands, feet, mouth," was the hardest for me to work on. I worked with duct tape.

So, the art process gave me permission to experience it, to deal with it, to process it, to take it away from a horrible memory, to transform that duct tape back into just duct tape.

Through counseling, I had to go through a process of saying "duct tape." I had to laugh about it, ask, "Why is it called duct tape? Is it d-u-c-k or what?" I had to play with it because anytime someone said, *duct tape* . . . You would not believe how many times it comes up in conversation. It is, like, so common.

While I was in the hospital, I decided I did not want to be fearful, inward, scared, and feel like a victim. I couldn't talk; my mouth was wired shut. I knew they were going to talk me into taking drugs, which I did not want to do. I didn't want to cover up any of my feelings. I wanted to feel them all; I wanted to be able to process them all. I didn't want to shy away in *any* way because I knew they would just keep coming up over and over in my mind as trauma. I wanted to deal with it head-on—there, then, now—and not delay it. Drugs, I knew, would do that. I was going to make decisions about my life that were positive and life-affirming. There was no reason for me to stay in that moment or keep reliving it over and over. I also decided I was going to talk about it a lot in order to take the shame out of it. He was not going to take anything else from me.

I grew up with a religious background but decided as an adult that I did not need it. But when I was in the hospital, I had visions. From my hospital bed, I could see the sky with all the clouds and the colors from the sun. It felt like I was in heaven. What I saw was so clear and beautiful. The clouds began to form hands that were warm and nurturing, and then I saw an image of a man, and I knew it was Jesus. But he was not the biblical Jesus—white with blonde hair—he was Arab looking. He faded and then the Mother and Child appeared. I knew when that happened that I had to believe. Then the heavens opened, and it looked like a star nebula. I went into it and saw a place like heaven where I heard chatter. This happened one month after 9/11 when the U.S. was invading Afghanistan. I was given a message that things were going to be okay, and that there was a battle raging between good and evil on earth and in heaven. The message was also that there was hope and that good would prevail. I believed I had been in a battle of good versus evil with Michael [her boyfriend].

One of the investigators on the case asked me if I believed in God. I said, "I do now." I always believed Jesus was an important man who lived on this earth and had a loving, wonderful message. He was in the same category as Muhammad and Buddha and any other image of what we call a presence, of God. There is a reason I am alive. How could I not change spiritually after experiencing something like this?

John Johannessen

On his way to work on July 18, 1997, John Johannessen listened to a Los Angeles radio news report that more than fifteen hundred people in LA County die each year from gunshots. In disbelief, his thoughts drifted toward their loved ones who suffer the grief and anguish of such losses. Feeling thankful that he lived in Orange County and didn't have to worry about those things, he was shocked when his wife called three hours later bringing the anguish to him: "Shanelle's been shot!" His beautiful twelve-year-old daughter had been shot through the head because a neighbor's gun had been left unsecured.

Hearing that your daughter has been shot—I cannot explain, when you hear something like that, what it does to you. It is the most shocking thing that rivets through you. I could tell my wife was serious when she told me, because she had kind of a shaky, low voice. I was like, "Oh my god! No way!" There are so many thoughts that come over your mind. I thought, *Okay, she got shot in the leg.*

I asked, "Where did she get shot?"

"She got shot through the neck and it went out the other side."

"Is she still alive?"

"Yes, but she is on life support, so hurry to the hospital."

The whole time you are thinking, *Oh my god, how can something like this happen? I move into a safe neighborhood . . .* and my

John Johannessen and his daughter Shanelle

Shanelle two weeks before the shooting
(photo by Schultz Bros. Photography)

other thoughts are, *Will I ever speak to her again and see her?* and then I am going back and forth: *Where did this gun come from? We do not have drive-by shootings.* And then I am like, *What if I never see her again?* These thoughts are going back and forth. It is like—you know how you see color? It is like it went into black and white; there was no color anymore. The day went kind of dark. It is the only way I can explain what I went through. It is like it just changed. It was horrible.

I am actually better at telling the story. I don't tell it very often, but I usually have a tough time with it because I relive it. I see it so clearly; it is like it happened yesterday. It is something you think about a lot. Even when you are at work and you are having your quiet time, you don't talk about it, but it is always on your mind. I don't think there is a day that goes by that you don't think about it in some way or another. As far as the shooting and what we went through, I never forget about it.

What was amazing was that when I got to the hospital, they would not let me see her. There were all the doctors and nurses and they were trying to save her and control the bleeding. I wanted to see her, so it seemed like forever. Finally, a nurse came out and said I could see her when they were taking her to the operating room. So they took us down this long, cold, dark hallway. It was like the hallway keeps getting longer as you are walking. Everything is such an incredible nightmare that you are living. It is horrifying. About ten minutes later, two doors opened and the stretcher came out with a little tiny girl lying on it covered in a white sheet with blood all over the place. They had her hooked up to a breather, and her eyes were closed. They stopped, and I kneeled down next to the thing they were pulling her around on and held her hand. She turned her head and looked at me, and I started crying.

I was like, "Baby I love you and you need to be strong and you hang in there. Please hang in there! Be strong." She couldn't talk, but she gave me a little tug with her finger on my hand, and I looked in her eyes and she was looking at me. It was like she

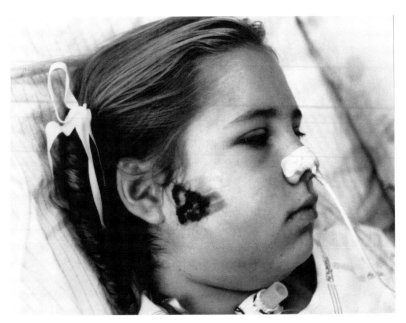

Shanelle at the hospital

was telling me *Okay*. She was going to be strong. I said, "Baby, I love you." I still did not know what happened. I did not know that she had been accidentally shot. I didn't care about what happened at that point.

I left it at that and went back upstairs and sat by her when she came out of surgery. I sat there for two weeks. I watched every little move on those monitors. Every now and then she would jump, and the monitor would kind of bounce on and off the screen. I think she relived it a few times while she was sleeping. I think she was dreaming it. I stayed right there making sure everything was okay. They had all these machines and tubes and lines and gears and stuff hooked up to her, keeping her alive.

As I sat there, I made a pledge that I would do whatever I could do to prevent this from happening to other people, just to make her survive. I thought, *I promise I will do that; just don't let her die.* And then her head started to swell from all of the trauma. She was not out of the woods yet. She had one surgery and was scheduled for another one because her jaw was still shattered.

I looked at the x-ray. You can see the path the bullet took. When it hit the jaw, it shattered the bones into all these little pieces, and they went all over inside her head. It took a big chunk of the jawbone out, and the rest that did not come out, it blew it apart. So it threw bone fragments all over inside of her. She survived one heck of a hit. It is just a miracle that she was even able to walk. It missed her spine by a quarter of an inch. It barely missed the jugular vein. The bullet went right between them.

Once she got out of the woods, on the third day, she started showing signs of improving. The swelling started to go down, and I was able to walk her. I held her up. She couldn't talk or anything; she was all wired shut, kind of a mess. I am walking my daughter through the hospital, and I am thanking God every step of the way that she is alive. I felt grateful. It is the most amazing thing to be so grateful after going through that, grateful that she is alive, and upset for the damage that she has had to go through.

She was released from the hospital two weeks after the shooting, but the damage goes on and on. She has had several reconstructive surgeries and she looks a lot better, but I never did get my little girl back. She changed and then the marriage fell apart. She had to grow up fast. She probably feels like she did. She was going to do a modeling thing, and they wouldn't take her, of course, because she had a damaged and disfigured face. She is still cute but when she smiles she has a crooked smile and you can see where the scar was.

The kids at school were hard with her. They would try and pretend that they were going to shoot her by pointing a finger at her, going *BANG*. Kids are mean. She went from a 4.0 down to a 2.6. Between that and the mean kids, I said, "What can we do to help you out, Shanelle?" She said, "I just want to quit school." She started getting suicidal on us. She was going downhill.

She used to go to schools and speak. Sometimes the local TV stations would go over and film her. She got burned out on it. She is twelve years old and now she is going around teaching about gun violence? It is like, stupid. She doesn't know anything about gun violence. And now we have to make her grow up really fast and do all this stuff when all she really wants is to be a kid. She said, "I don't want to do this anymore. I just want to forget it; I don't want to think about it anymore." It was a horrible experience. She didn't want to be exposed and be part of it. She wanted to move on with her life and try and be a kid.

Two doors opened and the stretcher came out with a little tiny girl lying on it covered in a white sheet with blood all over the place.

I feel anger about the way that it changed our lives so much. It changed our cozy little comfortable, happy situation that we had, and it never came back. We were just a normal family in just a normal neighborhood. We had normal friends. Everything was great—making money, life was normal, drove nice cars—not rich or anything like that, just normal. Within a few years, everything was scattered to the wind. It was just a crumbling block. Now things have mellowed out, and the kids have gone full circle and are doing okay. They still have their bad days, though. I am remarried, and my ex has gotten remarried. For me, I am a tough guy and I can handle it, but I am upset about what the kids went through. That's the part that is hard. It was an emotional drain on them and just a horrible thing for them to go through. That is where I am: upset that they had to experience this stupid, senseless thing.

Christie Toribara January 2004

Seventeen-year-old Craig was a talented athlete who was on a path to play collegiate soccer. He confided in his soccer coach his anxiety about not being called by Johns Hopkins University with an offer of a scholarship. His coach simply told him that not being called meant they were not interested. His mom, Christie, tried to tell him it wasn't true, but Craig insisted that his coach, who was well respected, was correct. One day after this conversation he committed suicide, and the day after his death, Johns Hopkins University called with a scholarship offer. Christie made a vow to her son and to God that she would do everything she could to stop this kind of tragedy. That is when she started the nonprofit organization SMILE (Students Mastering Important Lifeskills Education).

Craig had had his graduation pictures taken. We had picked out this graduation picture that many of his friends signed, and it is in our living room. There are things of Craig's and his sister's in his room. We use it as a guest room. It is not a shrine; we did not enshrine anything. I think that if you focus so much on the person who died, you can't let go, that you don't move forward with things you can do.

You say goodbye, but the reality hits later. Like, his wallet was on the table; none of us touched it for a long time. It takes awhile for it all to hit and for each person to adjust. One of the things that helped me, as far as even adjusting within the family, is knowing

Christie Toribara

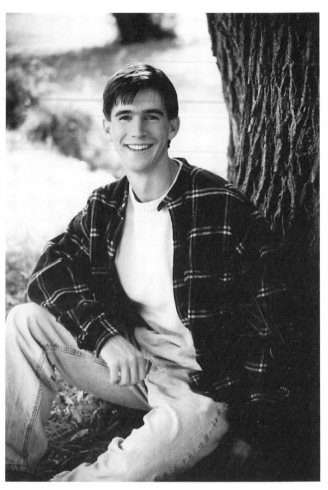

Christie's son Craig
(photo by Scott Jones)

that no two people will grieve the same way at the same time. Do not put blame on other people until you resolve your own issues. Know that you have dealt with everything, and only take *actions* personally. Do not lash out. Do not judge others for not grieving in the same way. You will not be at the same level at the same time, but that does not mean they are not grieving as deeply. I think that has helped as an adjustment.

After Craig's death I wanted to move out of our house, initially, and Ted, my husband, said no—he refused to move. And then it finally hit me, the realization that no matter where I was, the pain was going to be there. We stayed, and I am really glad we did, because there are so many memories of Craig, in so many ways, and I think I would have lost that. There is always that fear in the beginning—will I forget what the person looked like, will I forget events, will I remember certain things? It takes time for you to realize that yes, you will remember those things. Everywhere in the house there is something of him, whether it is intentional or unintentional.

After everyone left the service, Ted took me to a place to get me out of the house, to go have lunch or dinner. A year later, we went back to this place, and I said, "Oh, I've never been here." He said, "Yes, you have. This is where we came right after Craig died." I was finding, six months to a year later, that there were a lot of things I did not remember. I think all of us in the family have found that. Parts of that whole year were a blur. That was a very difficult thing. There is a lot I had to learn about grieving. I think about him everyday.

Soccer and Christmas decorations are what bring it back. Craig always knew he would get married and have a family, so he liked decorations for the holidays. His two favorites were Halloween and Christmas, and so every time we decorate for those two times, we think about him. He started a snow village for Christmas, and we completed it—the things he said he had wanted in it. We have ornaments—some that he made for the Christmas tree.

He loved Halloween; he had a great time with that, so we have some decorations that we bought for him that he knew he would keep long term. Holidays are different [now]. The first years, at least for me, were the most difficult. There still are those periods, though, [even] now, that I think, *He should be here*. It would be wonderful to know what he would be like at this point in his life, what he would be doing, what his interests were. It would be very, very difficult not to actually think of him.

My first day back at work, a woman came up to me and said, "Well, you know, ninety percent of people who have something happen like this get a divorce." I was not ready for that. I did not need to deal with that right [then]. I hope that will not happen, that we can work together as a family. Another woman came up to me and said, "Drug addict, wasn't he? Your kid was just a drug addict." I think they basically want to know or feel within themselves that what happened to you isn't anything that would affect their life, so they are safe.

The reality is that none of us are safe, because when somebody has committed suicide, it is them saying, *I have a tremendous amount of pain that is unresolved*. We need to change our views in society rather than condemn the person or make judgments. We need to be reaching out and helping, and dealing with issues whether they are depression, anxiety disorder, traumatic events, abuse, whatever. We need to deal with those social issues and help people take away suicide as how to resolve a problem.

I was very, very disappointed when I was watching *SNL* (*Saturday Night Live*) one night, and Jennifer Aniston had in her little comic sketch about committing suicide, and made it into a joke. Suicide is not a joke. I probably would not have reacted to this degree before. It hurts. And it makes me very frustrated with our entertainment media that they view suicide as some-thing to entertain with, either as a joke or without realizing the remembrance and pain that is inflicted, not understanding the pain that the people who commit suicide feel.

One person made a comment that Craig was just selfish. He

wasn't selfish. He was one of the most kind, giving people you could ever meet. I think the thing about those comments is that I *knew* he was not selfish, a drug addict, or an alcoholic, so I wanted to know why he committed suicide. That was the impetus that pushed me forward. I wanted to know *why*. What are the causes of suicide? How can we prevent it? What can we do? What are things that we as individual people can do to make a difference?

You do not know what takes a person to where they are.

I do not think I will ever be at peace with it. I do know we can change things, and I do know it is important to stand for what you believe and to make a difference. I strongly believe we can help people. I certainly have empathy, understanding, and probably more patience with people who have mental disorders, difficulties in life, and even people who are living on the street. You do not know what takes a person to where they are. And I do not think we can judge. I certainly cannot judge other people. Having boundaries is one thing, but certainly not judging. I probably did a fair amount before—not intentionally. I definitely have gained more understanding of people.

If I didn't know what I [now] know about suicide, I probably would be angry at Craig. There is a frustration, but I have a better understanding of his pain. Am I angry with him at this point? No. Were there points when I felt anger and frustration? Yes. But I don't know if it was at him or not being able to counteract what had happened to him.

Craig was determined to die. He had a backup to the gun. That shows his determination to end the pain. When he set his mind to something, he did it. He was like that all the way through his life. He had turned in all of his assignments the day before. The idea that all kids [contemplating suicide] are going to show this path—grades start falling, getting into drugs, getting promiscuous—that is not always the case. This is something we as a society need to wake up to. The stereotype is not accurate. It may happen that way, but it may not, and we need to be looking at other kids. We need to be aware that these kids are being stereotyped, and deal with them as individuals. The one thing Craig said on a continual basis during that last part was, "What is the use; what is the point." That was a clear indication that he was giving up.

One thing we have been fortunate about is that he had good relationships with his friends, and they have become our friends, not through him as he was as a boy, but now directly as our friends. The young woman who was his girlfriend is very close to us, as are several of his other friends. That has been a wonderful gift. That is one thing I have to say about Craig—he chose very wisely in friendships. He chose wonderful people as friends.

I feel Craig in everything I say and do in the work we do with SMILE. He is certainly an inspiration; he was a wonderful person, and he gave so much of himself. He used to always say, "Why are people so inhumane to each other? Because I do not understand." He was very supportive of other people, caring and understanding. So we are trying to do the same, not only in the respect that we want to stop suicide and destructive acts, but also taking the step to be humane and caring to one another because he was that kind of person. He is definitely an inspiration.

Mary Leigh Blek October 2003

One early morning in July of 1994, Mary Leigh and her husband Charlie got a call that forever changed their lives. Their twenty-one-year-old-son Matthew had been shot and killed by three teenagers toting cheap handguns in a New York robbery. At the time of this interview, nine years after her son's murder, Mary Leigh had become a national leader successfully lobbying for legislation to reduce gun violence in America.

I am a reader so I immediately started reading all the grief books: How to grieve. I thought I would wake up the next day and I would be dead. I didn't know how I could live. Here I was alive, and I had two other children that were alive and needed me, and I had to be there for them. Sometimes I thought what a relief it would be to die, to not have to have the pain because it is such a motivating factor for all of us who have lost someone. The pain is excruciating. I once described it as, *You know when you set your hand on a hot stove, and you know how painful it is?* The way I was able to keep my hand off that hot stove was to keep myself busy. Thank God I stumbled onto this whole gun violence prevention issue because it allowed me to not let my hand rest. I didn't rest that hand on that stove because when you are tired, your hand falls and you have that singe, and the pain is just awful. I wouldn't [wish] it on my worst enemy. It is an awful pain. To see my kids in pain, and see Charlie's pain . . . it is just awful. In my reading, I heard about how parents who go through this agonizing

Mary Leigh Blek

Mary Leigh's son Matthew

experience, their marriage often breaks up. I do not know if it is a myth or not, but I wasn't going to let it happen. I had already lost a son. I didn't want to lose my husband. I would read to Charlie because that is what he likes. We made a pact that this was not going to tear our marriage or family apart. We have only gotten stronger—a tighter marriage.

Some people prefer the word *survivor*. I don't care; if you feel like a survivor, then be a survivor. I feel like a victim. I am just as much a victim as when Matthew was first shot, as I am the day I die. I will still feel like a victim because I lost Matthew.

I know that many victims use the word *healing*. I never feel like I was sick. That model works for many victims. Some people feel very strongly that they are a survivor; they have lived and gotten through this. They are not going to be victimized; they are a survivor. I respect and honor that. What I feel in my mind is that I have learned coping skills to get through and be able to go on and do the things that I want to in my life and for the life of my children. That is how I feel. I do not feel like I have had this healing, I just feel like I have learned some good skills for helping cope with my loss. But my loss is just as much a loss as it was nine years ago, as it is today. I do feel that Matt has given me a lot of guts.

Matthew was killed in June and it wasn't until a bit later in February that we went back for the sentencing hearing of the boys who were with the shooter. I remember it being so important to me that I tell these two boys how important Matthew was to us but also to tell them about Matthew. I wanted to make this real to them so I had prepared eight pages of remarks, and Charlie did the same. I really worried that those words would get stuck in my throat. That is one of the things that I thought was very empowering for me because I was able to get through that. I said everything to those boys that I wanted to say, and I am very grateful for that. It also showed me that I can speak on this issue and say what I needed so desperately to say. As the tears were coming, they kept dripping off my chin and I kept going. I didn't stop and I told our story. That was very empowering for me. I am grateful that in New York and so many other states that you are allowed to do that.

Our first public meeting was the following June. I was in New York with my daughter attending the trial for the shooter. Of course Charlie did not want to go, I respect that. But I had to be there. So we sat through the trial. At the end of the trial he was found guilty, he will probably serve, he *could* serve life but they figure probably about twenty-five years. The kid was only fifteen.

I was quite disturbed about the gun because they had tossed it, and I wanted them to find that gun. I didn't want anyone else to find that gun and use it. The DA looked at me and said, "That gun; it really is a non-issue. There are so many guns here that it is no problem finding a gun. Don't be obsessive about that gun. Kids can get a gun very easily."

It started me to thinking. Because I was interested in learning more about this issue, I wrote to this kid and asked him where he got his gun. I said I would like to write, and he wrote me back and denied that he shot Matt. But I knew he did. He said how people get guns is that they go down to the South and put the guns in the trunk and then they bring them into the hood. They sell them out of the trunk. It is just as true today and fifteen-year-olds know about it. Now I was going to do something about it.

I knew Matthew had been killed with a Saturday night special so I started working with a group of others who were working to ban Saturday night specials in California. I remember going with Charlie up to Sacramento for the first time to testify at a public safety committee. I truly believed that I would just go up there and we would tell our story and they would say, "I am so glad, Mr. and Mrs. Blek, that you came to tell us about this problem." I had no idea. Of course it didn't get out of committee so we continued [going] back to Sacramento until we got a ban on Saturday night specials in 1999.

I have raised three fifteen-year-olds. I know that fifteen-year-olds do stupid, dumb things. Certainly I want to hold the three of them accountable and responsible, and have consequences for their behavior. My anger was directed at society. *We* are the ones; the adults are responsible for providing a safe and nurturing environment, and I know these kids did not come from a safe and nurturing environment. I also know that our gun industry, with the complacency of the general public, has allowed the easy access and availability of guns.

That is how I have approached this in relationship to forgiveness of Joseph—Matt's killer. I feel that it is not my place to forgive Joseph. That is between Joseph and his family and his God. That is not my role, and perhaps it belongs to Matthew. It just does not feel like it is my role to forgive Joseph, and it never has.

I'd look at the sunset and I'd say *that is beautiful,* **but I couldn't feel it. I could see it but I couldn't feel it.**

The only thing is that I did feel a connection with one young boy [one of two charged as accomplices] and I did reach out to him. We exchanged two letters and I said to him that in order for us to continue what I hope will be some sort of connection is that we be honest with each other. I even asked him if he likes to read. All my kids are huge readers and I thought maybe I could open something up. I had all kinds of thoughts about how I could touch this kid, but I wasn't going to do it if he was going to be dishonest with me. The letter I got from him said that that wasn't going to happen. So the relationship never happened. I am glad I made the effort. What he said was very prophetic. It opened my eyes when he said they go and get the guns in the South and bring them up and sell them out of their trunks in the hood. It helped me focus my attention on gun violence prevention and gun control, and I was very grateful to have this work. It helped me to keep my hand off that hot stove until I had better coping skills to deal with the loss.

I remember the first few years feeling that there was this filter in our life, and *I do not think I am ever going to feel joy.* But today I feel there is potential for me. I'd look at the sunset and I'd say *that is beautiful,* but I couldn't feel it. I could see it but I couldn't feel it. I am starting to feel again.

We are expecting a grandchild, and I used to be crazy about babies. I want to bring every ounce of joy with this new grandchild. But there is also the fear. To love someone so much, the pain of losing them . . . but I am ready to walk that walk again. I think.

It is not that I don't love my own kids; there is something about a new life. I have already invested in my kids, now I am going to have this new entity, and I want to give it all my love and attention, and that is a risk. I know how it hurts to lose somebody, and I am much more fearful about the safety of my children. That is a bit frightening.

I thought I lived a very charmed life. I had a wonderful life and tragedy was just not coming my way. Even when my mom died of breast cancer—she was my best friend—I was able to reinvest in my family, stabilize, and keep going. But Matthew's death . . . just shakes me to my core.

Robin Shanafelt April 2005

One warm June evening in 1997 after going to the Opera, Robin and her husband Ken were walking back to their car when Ken was struck in the head and killed by a stray bullet fired by a teen during a dispute five blocks away. Left to raise three children, and consumed with sadness, Robin worked to negotiate a plea bargain (from an original sixty-year sentence to twenty-three years) for the man convicted of killing her husband.

We were walking hand in hand. One second he was standing there, and then he's down—dead. I didn't know what had happened. It's not like there was a bunch of blood. He starts to fall and there is this huge flash of light. I didn't know what was going on. When the police were doing their investigation, I was trying to describe this flash of light to them. I told them, "I think it came from over there . . ." but it was right here next to me. I think it was spirit, Ken's spirit—that kind of quick exit. I tried to help him and put a cloth over the wound but didn't realize that he was already dead.

They took me in a police car to the police station, which was a couple of blocks away. I didn't want to drive home and didn't know how I was going to get home. I wanted to call my Dad but he was out of town. So I called my mom who was babysitting the kids. It was the hardest call I have ever had to make. I told her, "Don't freak out but . . ." At around midnight this really nice compassionate policeman drove me home. I didn't wake up

Robin Shanafelt

Robin and her husband Ken

the kids when I got home but knew I had a lot to do. I became really focused and was surprised by my inner strength. I called my best friend who came over immediately, and then I called Ken's family and my family. They all started coming over the next morning.

The next morning I told the kids. That was really hard. I do not remember much of that but my kids do. My son Bryan really regrets that he and Ken got into a fight before we left that night. He wanted to come with us and had complained that it was unfair that we got to go out. My youngest daughter now feels cheated because she was only four and does not have that many memories of her dad.

For the next year and a half there was all this business with charging Daniel DeJesus [the shooter]. Many people wanted the full sentence. At the beginning I went along with it but then changed my mind because it did not seem fair. Two weeks after Ken's death a girl was shot and killed in North Portland. She was walking with gang members and she was black. The guy who shot her was only charged with a misdemeanor when Ken's shooter was looking at sixty-some-odd years. I felt immense pressure to hate and to want the maximum penalty for Ken's killer, but it didn't feel right. When I found out who the shooter was I remember thinking, "Great, that is the guy I am going to hate and blame."

There was a plea bargain offered, and I wanted to take it because I didn't want to go to trial and I didn't want Daniel DeJesus to have the max sentence. So I wrote a letter to the DA [district attorney] and to everyone saying what I wanted, and I think it really upset people. I met with the DA and said, "This girl was killed the same way as Ken. If you can explain to me why her killer only gets a few years and Ken's killer gets sixty years, and explain why that is fair, then I will go along with what you want." The next day they agreed to the plea.

During all this time I was having to deal with the DA and fight to reduce the sentence, I felt really sad. For us it's been about loss and sorrow and grief. I think when you hold on to the hate and anger it shields you from being able to really feel any form of feeling sad. That's mostly what I felt—sadness. I cried all the time.

There was a moment when I decided the direction I was going to take. It started when I took my son to the doctor because he had been sick. The doctor knew about Ken's death and I told him how they had found the guy who did it. So I was telling the doctor about it, and he was asking me some questions. "Well, the kid who shot Ken did not do it on purpose right? I mean he was not trying to kill or hurt Ken, right?" And I was like, "Yeah, he was not trying to kill Ken, it was random."

It got me thinking.

Then that Father's Day weekend I decided I wanted to get away from everything. Father's Day is hard. I took the kids to the beach along with a friend and her kids. I just wanted to get away and let the kids play in the sand while I sobbed on the beach. We went to a secluded area away from everyone. I just remember there being all kinds of nuclear families everywhere; lots of families with a mom and dad along with their kids. So we found a place and put our blanket down and got settled. Then over the hill came a Hispanic single mom with her kids and she put her blanket right next to ours. There was plenty of room on the beach and she didn't need to be right next to us. I really wanted to be alone but she asked if it would be okay if they sat there with us so we could help each other watch over the kids. I realized that we were not so different. I could not hate her or hate an entire race. I realized that anger and hate was not the way to go.

I didn't want this experience to make my kids hateful and fearful. I didn't want them to be scared to go downtown or scared of Hispanics or anything like that. The priority has been getting them through this without hating the world—and without the fear of random bullets flying through the air. I am their role model and knew I had to show them that the world was not scary, and that they didn't need to hate. So far I think it has worked. They aren't fearful and they're really nice kids.

The biggest lesson I have learned is about the absolute power of optimism and just really looking at the glass as half-full, and how so many times every day, big and little, you have the opportunity to see the glass as half-full or half-empty. It just feels so much better to look at the bright side.

I have learned the importance of network, really nurturing your female relationships—your relationships with girls. I mean, I didn't know what I would have done without this network of other mothers that have helped to raise my kids and helped me be supportive of myself. The same kind of group has created family. We continue to be best of friends. The kids have grown up together. I didn't have as strong of a network before Ken's death. I had relationships with women but didn't really need them.

The priority has been getting our kids through this without hating the world—and without the fear of random bullets flying through the air.

The first anniversary—that was weird. I had a little ritual with the kids that night but I thought that I needed to spend the night sort of reflecting. So I took a tent and my dog and went to a little campground, pitched my little tent, and I was going to do some journaling and reflection. I got scared and I was hungry because all I brought was s'mores makings and I ended up staying until about 4:00 in the morning. I intended to do this spiritual thing and it just turned out to be me scared in the woods—scared and hungry.

I was pretty much raised kind of an atheist. I always had questions and I always kind of knew *something* but didn't really know *what*, didn't really have a formal path. For me, religion or any spiritual practice was kind of a weakness. It was the opposite of intellect. After Ken's death, that first year was hugely spiritual for me. Part of it was a self-preservation thing but it was so rich that I can't just call it a preservation thing. I say that because if I were to really believe that that was it, ashes to ashes, and then it was over—well that was too big to really accept. But I didn't have to because that spiritual relationship was so rich that I couldn't discount it. So that year I was looking more seriously for more structure. I was having this experience; I knew I was officially connecting to something. Part of it was Ken, I really feel like I can ask Ken a question and get an answer. Is that just that I knew him so well that I have his answer? It is not like I hear him, "Well, Robin . . . " But I know his answers. And that does not happen as much now. In that first year it was like he was still there, and it was really cool. It was pretty much in my head. I just never felt like he was so *gone* I do not feel him present like I did before, sometimes more than other times. I do not feel his spirit like a separate thing—like he is sitting on the couch—it is more like an internal thing. It is all so hokey.

My advice to others? I think you don't have to feel the way that society and culture and the DA and the family feel. You don't have to feel the same. You are not crazy if you don't. It's okay to have a different experience than the majority. I recognize that it is kind of a minority sort of experience. It is okay and it's absolutely healthy. There are like-minded people. You might not run into them, you might have to look a little harder, but you are going to run into a whole bunch of "parents of murdered children" groups. There will be plenty of angry people who will say that you have every right to hate and to feel all that and to want justice and burn and death penalty. There will be no shortage of those people. The glass is half-full and those kinds of people are not quite as frequent.

Ken's killer got twenty-two years in prison. A couple of years ago I was asked to serve on a task group to develop protocol for a "serious and violent offender victim mediation dialogue" kind of thing and develop for the state of Oregon just what the protocol is for offender/victim dialogue. It is victim initiated because they want to have some kind of conversation. So I have not communicated with him even though I have been a part of the structure of how it can happen. Someday—maybe. I wish him well, all the best. I hope more than anything that he doesn't and hasn't continued to be self-destructive, although, prison is not a healthy place for anybody. I was not there for the sentencing. I went to the beach. He didn't mean to do it [to kill Ken]. He meant to kill someone that night, he really did. There had been a fight, and the people who were involved in the fight were running away. He took the gun from his buddy, and he shot at the people who were running away.

I went to a conference, Murder Victim's Families for Reconciliation. It was the first time ever that I had shared the same space with three hundred to four hundred people who had lost loved ones to either murder or something like that. They had shared similar experiences and it was the most powerful experience [to be there with them]. You are not alone.

Liz Julee

Alcohol, depression, and guns defined the family trag-edies that marred Liz's younger years in Kentucky. By the time she was thirty-four, five family members had died from gun violence. Her uncle was shot and killed in a bar fight. Her favorite cousin died while cleaning his hunting rifle. After a couple of suicide attempts and some time in a state hospital, her mom shot and killed herself. Her aunt shot and killed her abusive husband. A few years later, that aunt's sons got into an argument, and one of her sons shot and killed her other son.

Liz resolved not to have guns be a part of her life, but the lasting effects of family violence lived in Liz through depression. Sixty-three at the time of this in-terview, she had lived through a bad divorce, a seri-ous suicide attempt, and intermittent depression. She had learned to get help at the first sign of serious de-pression, and to use her experience, knowledge, and passion to encourage others to keep guns out of their homes. Her experience taught her that easy access to firearms leads to nothing but heartache.

I grew up in a rural area—moderately poor family but not in any distress. We always had food but there was no extra money to go to the high school football games sort of thing. I grew up in a dif-ferent era. I didn't grow up in a city where there's probably more crime and violence—so things that happened where I grew up

Liz Julee

involving guns were generally more accidental. I never heard of anybody being shot with a handgun. I was on the farm and my hometown was a population of about two thousand. That's very different than, say, someone in Portland, Oregon, which is a fairly mild and diverse city. Here, in Portland, I didn't know anyone who had guns in the home but I still saw the guns when I went back to Kentucky where people hunted. That supplemented our food supply—rabbits, squirrels, and quail. There were five young deaths in this family and it was not a [stereotypical] ghetto family. It was small town, farm people, churchgoing people.

I have learned that I don't want guns in my home, I don't want them in my kids' homes, [and] I want to work to take as many guns out of homes as possible. I want to work to educate people about gun violence and the lethality of guns. I think guns—you don't get any second chance with guns, for the most part. Guns are more likely to be lethal than any other method [of self-protection]. Most of those suicides would be from guns in the home.

I know a lot of people say it's not the guns, it's the people. I definitely know my cousin wouldn't have been killed without a gun. The uncle—probably beat up bad, maybe knifed, I don't know. The story of the uncle and aunt . . . you know, why didn't they get a divorce years ago? She was probably scared to death of him, you know, the domestic violence happened. This is the trouble. Why have it [a gun] in the home? I guess something like that triggers back to my mother. Why didn't they take the guns out of the home? Because nobody thought of that.

When I was thirty-one, I went through a very bad divorce, and I became very depressed. I also had a suicide attempt, with an overdose. It was a serious attempt. I was in a coma for four days after. I was very much at peace with myself at the time I did

Liz's mom Helen

the overdose. I had decided that *I'm going to do this; I'm going to take these pills. I intend to kill myself.*

Depression must run in us, in our lineage. I drove around all morning and screamed and yelled at God. I came back and I thought *I'm at peace with myself, this is what I want to do, this is why I want to do it*—I did it. When I woke up, I remembered people from work being there off and on, kind of hazy, but I woke up. I decided then, *I am going back to school. I am going to beat this.* But whatever that experience was, I had the opportunity to come back from the brink, [the opportunity] that my mother didn't have.

If you're in this depression and you're being treated but you still aren't improving, you begin to wonder how long will it go on; will I ever be any better. Am I more of a detriment to my children being here than not being here. I came to the point where I fully understood what was going on with my mother at that time—which was different than going to her funeral, which was very devastating to me. Well, maybe my mom's suicide gave me permission, that [killing myself] was an option. I don't know. Also I think it gave me the understanding of where she must have been. I don't know. I think my own experience made me know how people who are thinking about suicide must be feeling, or even that it's a cry for help.

I know a lot of people say it's not the guns, it's the people. I definitely know my cousin wouldn't have been killed without a gun.

How did all these gun deaths in my family impact me? Well, I never wanted to fight. Fighting and anger were really bad and maybe to my own detriment for a while about anger, until I learned, probably in my early thirties: it's okay to be angry. This is about how you *express* it.

Thirty years later or so, when my current husband and I were moving in together, he had a gun—a very antique gun that was his grandfather's. He brought it and was showing it to me. I just started crying. It was, *Why would that have come up then?* He said, "I don't want to get rid of it," but he broke it down and boxed it up, which really was very compassionate.

I regretted very much that I was never able to develop an adult to adult relationship with my mother at that age.

Another thing . . . when I was forty-eight and then when I became forty-nine and I had outlived my mother, that was another point that really struck me. I'm sixty-three now. All of this life that I have now, all those years I have, she never had.

John Oerter

In 2003, John Oerter suffered an unimaginable loss: his son-in-law killed his two-and-half-year-old granddaughter, a six-month old girl, and himself. The drama that ended in such tragedy began when his stepdaughter, Heidi, and her husband, Howard, lost their first child, an eleven-day-old boy to a virus. A year later she gave birth prematurely to Madeline. It was then that Heidi complained that Howard was abusing her, and they separated. By manipulating the system Howard gained custody of Madeline. He later met a woman who gave birth to their child Elizabeth. Howard's life spun out of control after his girlfriend (Elizabeth's mother) was killed in a car accident. Fearing pressure that he would lose custody of Madeline and Elizabeth he took his handgun, put a pillow up to Madeline, and shot and killed her. He then shot and killed Elizabeth while she lay in her crib, before killing himself.

John and his wife, Lucia, found strength in each other and in their faith as Presbyterian ministers as they helped Heidi recover from such loss.

Madeline, was petite, blonde, blue-eyed, cute, very alive and aware—just beautiful. Quite verbal, early. Just the way little girls do, they love to be in the middle of things and have the social interaction: play with her toys, ask questions, bring you stuff. One of the things Lucia and I still do is, when a stoplight changes she [Madeline] would [say], "Go-go-go!" So sometimes when we are seeing each other distracted—*Go-go-go!* And then try not to cry.

John Oerter

She was two-and-a-half when she was murdered.

I had just gotten to the truck after a meeting and called Lucia and could tell that she was sad. She said, "John, Howie has murdered Madeline and himself." And we just wept. I remember being that sad when my parents died. I don't ever remember being that angry. I was not surprised or shocked when I found out. I was really sad, that weird kind of self-recrimination and frustration. I mean, we knew he was dangerous and we knew he was weird. I know enough about narcissism to know that [for Howard it was] *I'll take my ball and go home* and not get in the way, and that's essentially what it was. *If I can't have them nobody can have them.* But we'd been working really hard to show the powers that be that the guy and his family were dangerous people.

Howie is not hard to understand: narcissistic little mean son of a bitch. *They are my things, you can't have them.* Well, child of God, they are not things, they are people: God's interesting, ironic mercy. I had for months or a year been praying everyday that Madeline's precious little soul wouldn't be warped by him.

I hadn't had any thought about, *God why did you do that to Madeline?* It was Howie's doing. I know enough about narcissism to know that sometimes it is truly wicked. I think it's important with anger to be honest—to be honest with your emotions and honest with your situation. When you're angry, it helps the perspective and the constructive action if you discharge the physical energy. Lots of folks do that self-destructively, and that's just stupid. For my anger, I'd work out, I'd hit things, I'd use the stick. We also had sledgehammers and axes, and that's a really satisfying thing. I sometimes will take the physical energy and make something. I make pipes to smoke, you just carve away the wood. There's something very focused about it. I know I'm

John's granddaughter Madeline

taking the energy and doing something with it. It just discharges the energy.

It also really helps me to know that anger is secondary to the primary emotion. In this case it's loss and grief, and so you try and make some peace with the loss. I mean, you can't change it. She's gone. I think our faith tells us we'll meet again, and in some way she's up there rooting for us, which is great. I think that's pretty cool. She's going, *Go-go-go!*

Heidi lived with us for six to nine months after. We just kind of sheltered her. I remember making a batlike thing out of a shovel handle and putting big gnarly black screws in the end and getting her cardboard boxes to hit. We'd be talking for a minute, she'd get sad, and then she'd just disappear and I'd hear in the back yard, *whack, whack, whack*. So part of my training in therapy, I did anger—getting angry and physical without hurting yourself or others. So she would destroy boxes.

I remember being that sad when my parents died. I don't ever remember being that angry.

It's just awful. Helping *her* helps. I don't remember ever being that sad, and I sort of know how to grieve. But I don't ever remember being that angry at social services, furious at Howie, angry at myself for not being an effective protector. I kind of let that go after a while. I remember one dream. [I] sat straight up in bed and woke myself up. The dream was [that] we had this one circular house with a courtyard in the middle and the outside windows were locked and Howard was running around the outside of the house trying to get in. I was pacing him inside and along the way I picked up a hammer and as he burst in the front door I sunk the hammer into his forehead and killed him. Just went *AWGHHHH!* And that's how I woke up. After that it was better.

I'm pretty sad right now. The anger seems to be less and less, which is very nice. It was markedly different after the dream. There was something zingy about being angry enough to . . . We joke about it: *Well if he didn't do it himself, we would have stood in line to do it ourselves.* Well that's not entirely a joke. I think all of us would have come up short of it, but if he were accessible in the flesh, I probably would have hurt him. Him killing himself gave us something. I think it's a coward's way out. I disdain that, although again, it's him manipulating the system and taking himself out of any—kind of *You can't do that to me either, see?* The gift is that he's not here and he's not affecting anybody; he's not affecting our lives except in retrospect. If he had hung around, just the level of my anger would have tempted me to complicate my life in a way that would not have been helpful. So all in all, I'm pretty glad he took himself.

I had occasions to think about what Jesus meant about forgiveness. Is it a blanket *Be nice to everyone no matter what?* It clearly isn't. Jesus said, *Don't throw your pearls in front of swine because they'll stomp them into the mud and then they'll turn and rip you with their fangs.* Jesus talked a lot about clear boundaries. The resistance we are to make is probably not a militant one but one of love and prayer and action.

The court system is such a hard thing 'cause it just keeps the pain and loss stuck. And grief is cyclical: you do this and then you do it again and do it again. It's kind of like a spiral staircase; hopefully you're at a different level, but the court process goes on for so long that it keeps you stuck right there.

Generally justice doesn't strike me that much. That comes from my understanding of grace, and it really is a gut-deep understanding that we all need God's grace. The other thing I've noticed [is that] they say *Justice has been done* and *I've got closure* or *I can put it behind me now.* I think that one is true. I don't think the first two are true because in our nature we want to have revenge, and we want to balance the scales. But what happens if we do that: we lose some important part of our humanity, and it's real hard to get that back. The whole legal system is based on justice and balance, although it doesn't function that way actually. So the very premise of getting well by getting legal satisfaction—it's not the way the human soul was built. So I don't see very many people who put a lot of energy into getting settlements, getting justice done, getting revenge through the punishment in the legal system. I don't think that that really helps people get better. I think there is a way, like a funeral, saying *This is done and over. We got the judgment. That was the process and now is life.* That part can function effectively.

My advice to others is: use your pain and loss to deepen your faith and deepen your relationships [with] those who are precious to you.

You asked me, "How is your marriage?" because you know very well that marriages disintegrate over something like this. For years I had up on my wall, "Make the most of your misery; it may not last forever," acknowledging that there are certain kinds of learning and growth that only happen in times of great distress. So if you find yourself in it, find a way to use it to deepen your faith and deepen your love and your relationships. Get into a community—it's very had to do that alone. Thankfully there are some good groups that are aware and can help you. Surround yourself with people who know that.

Bobbie Peyser

Bobbie Peyser's forty-one-year-old daughter, Wendy Waggner, was a firefighter in Santa Fe, New Mexico. In July 1997, she was abducted in Santa Fe. Two days later, her body was found in an Oklahoma field. She'd been shot three times and set on fire. Bobbie and her husband, Art, were devastated and struggled to remain calm and in control as they participated in the investigation, funeral, and memorial services. What follows is a week and a day in the life of a mother whose only daughter was murdered.

It was **Monday evening,** and my mom was having dinner with us when the phone rang. It was my brother, Barak [from Santa Fe], and I greeted him with warmth and love. His words filled me with astonishment and disbelief. Wendy, my beloved daughter, was missing. My first reaction was one of denial. This could not be. *She must be out shopping with the money from the moving sale she held over the past weekend, or maybe she went to see her fiancé in another state.* Maybe, maybe, maybe. No, she had not shown up for work, and nobody had seen her all day. This phone call began to feel scary and made me anxious. What would I say to my mother, my son Warren? Where was Wendy? I sat down at the table and casually told Art and Mom what my brother had said. They agreed that Wendy was off doing her own thing. Later that evening I called my son, Warren. I held back my tears of fear as we talked about the disturbing news.

Bobbie Peyser and her husband Art

Bobbie and her daughter Wendy

Tuesday morning. Now I was starting to panic, to feel fear and alarm. *What has happened to Wendy? This is not like her.* Wendy's friends and fellow firefighters in Santa Fe had flyers made with her picture and a picture of her truck that had disappeared with her. They posted them all over town. I remember taking a shower and thinking, *This is a safe place; no one will hear me,* and I started to sob, yell, and scream. I beat my fists on the tile wall until I was exhausted. Then I lay down in the bathtub in a fetal position and let the water pour over me, trying to wash away the pain, helplessness, and confusion that was racing through my body. Nothing helped. I felt limp and bewildered. This was like a dream to me.

Wednesday. I had been up all night trying to be lucid and rational, packing some clothes, getting ready to fly to Santa Fe. I had to be there; being at home was too frustrating. Art drove me to the airport, stopping to pick up my son on the way. When we met him, we just held each other. We each wanted to feel the strength and stability that the other had to give. There were many spoken words of encouragement and many times of shared silence as my son and I flew to Santa Fe to meet the unknown. I felt tense and unnerved not knowing what news there would be when we arrived at my brother's office.

Thursday. There was still no news, not even from the private investigator. I sat in my brother's office waiting, waiting, waiting. I felt useless, like the paper in the wastebasket, while he kept busy on the phone talking to local police, sheriff's office, state police, the FBI, and our private investigator. Later in the afternoon, Wendy's father arrived from the East Coast. We could do nothing but share our fear, worry, and anxiety. Now I had something to do. I could take care of my ex-husband.

Finally, there was a call from the private investigator telling us he had some unpleasant news. We sat holding each other as he told us about a Jane Doe matching Wendy's description, who had been found in Oklahoma. We sat there in a state of shock, filled with disbelief and horror. This could not be true. I felt overwhelmed by a force beyond my control. I started to yell, "Call her dentist! Call her dentist!" She had had a lot of work done, and this would prove that Jane Doe was not Wendy. A conference call with the dentist and the coroner in Oklahoma confirmed that, indeed, Jane Doe was Wendy Waggner. The room became silent, and then we all started to wail and cry. I could not accept the reality of what I had just heard. I felt weak and unsteady. I wanted to throw up, run and hide, pull the covers over my head, anything that would ease the pain, the trauma, the knowledge that my daughter had been murdered and her body driven to another state and burned. I was in a state of collapse. But I could not collapse. I had to move forward to take care of all the details yet to be done.

I called Art and again broke down as his emotions overflowed through the phone. I asked him to be with my mother when I called her with the sad news. Now I was getting into the swing of things, taking care of business. In a way, this was my salvation—contacting family and friends, making arrangements, and thinking about what to wear to the memorial service. *Keep busy, keep busy, keep busy. I'll get through it all if I just keep busy.*

Friday. More packing, more people, more decisions. Support, support, support. Everyone who arrived, after the initial hugs and tears, gave support, be it emotional, physical, or just being there to say, "I love you, and I loved Wendy." Finally, Art arrived. I clung to him like ivy to a wall. I didn't want to let go. He was my rock. I felt more secure now that he was by my side.

It was a day of business—making decisions, acting brave, greeting people who came from far and wide, comforting friends and firefighters who couldn't believe one of their comrades had fallen. Escaping to the bathroom was the only way I could get in touch with my own emotions. I had to deal with lawyers for the closing of Wendy's house that she had sold [a few days before her disappearance] as well as the funeral home and the decision to have Wendy's body cremated.

Supervising the dismantling of her home was a very unpleasant task. Everything that anyone touched brought memories and tears. Family and friends all pitched in to help. Everyone took something to remind him or her of Wendy. Decisions, decisions, decisions. Thank God for Valium.

Wendy had planned a going away party for herself [after her

house sold]. We turned this party into a gathering of family and friends to remember and honor her. It is a New Mexican tradition to have a table honoring the deceased on which special trinkets and mementos are placed and candles lit in memory. As this was Friday night, I asked to light the first candle. I took Wendy's *Shabbat* candlesticks that her grandmother had given her, and sang the blessing. I was told that this was the most sorrowful and saddening sound that those gathered had ever heard. I set the mood for the evening of sharing memories, tears and hugs, and silent remembrances.

I am not angry with God nor with Wendy for leaving me. I am just angry.

Saturday. Sitting on the floor in Wendy's bedroom holding clothing, laughing at her little bikinis and bathing suits, had a sobering effect on me. Sorting through closets and drawers, I felt grateful to be able to touch and smell all of Wendy's personal belongings. It was like having her back for a few minutes. I put aside many articles of clothing that I wanted for myself, including her very expensive cowboy boots. When I feel lonely and sad now, I put on one of her outfits. The bracelet of hers that I wear I have not taken off since I found out that she was murdered.

Saturday afternoon. Family and close friends met in the rabbi's office to remember, share, and cry, all of us wanting to talk and bring Wendy back. Arrangements had to be made for the memorial service at the temple on Sunday. When it was all done, I felt warm and comfortable, as if I was cradled in the rabbi's arms. How appreciative I felt that he had been a part of our life in the past. I felt secure in his words of guidance and direction. These words were like a beacon in the dark unknown.

Sunday. I was going to a memorial service for my daughter. I did not even have a chance to say goodbye or see her for the last time. All I had was a Ziploc bag of ashes. I hurt, I was tense, and I was powerless to change what was. At least sitting in the temple allowed me to feel somewhat peaceful and serene. The tears stopped for a while as I listened to the rabbi, the *chazzan* [cantor], the eulogies, and my own voice singing "Eli, Eli."

When we arrived at my brother's home after the service, I found a wooden box. This triggered a memory of Orthodox Jews sitting on a wooden box without shoes to sit *shiva*. I decided I needed to do this for myself. Reverting to an old custom gave me solace. I felt rooted to my Jewishness. I felt reverent and respectful to myself and to Wendy.

Monday. It was only one week after that shocking phone call from my brother, and it was the day for the public memorial at the main fire station. This was to be a ceremony with full honors for Wendy. Sitting in the front row with hundreds of people behind me, I felt unreal, as if everything was an illusion. I wanted to scream and strike out. I felt explosive, as if I was going to erupt, and I expected to see pieces of me flying in all directions. There was and is a hole in me that hurts terribly. The service had fire units from all around the surrounding area all draped in black with signs saying, "We Love You Wendy." There were bagpipes leading the procession of black-arm-banded firefighters. I felt very solemn and grim as I watched the sad, teary faces walk by me. There were more eulogies, speeches, poems, and tears. I came to realize how much Wendy was going to be missed by her community and all the people whose lives she had touched. I was overwhelmed by the outpouring of love and respect that all these people had for Wendy.

This day was the hardest yet. I am not angry with God nor with Wendy for leaving me; I am just angry. But at this time, my anger turned to rage, which was like a deep intense fury. I wanted to get my hands on Wendy's killer and tear him apart, and all I could do was cry. The tolling of the bell for a fallen firefighter left me devastated.

Tuesday. This was the day to pack up Wendy's house and head for home. Her death has no ending. It will always be with me—awake as I think about her and sleeping when I dream about her. I am thankful and proud that I had a daughter who loved people, and gave so much to our world with her love and compassion.

Rick Bath March 2007

Rick taught and coached at Columbine High School for nineteen years. His best friend and fellow teacher, Dave Sanders, was killed when two Columbine students opened fire in the school cafeteria and library, killing twelve and injuring twenty-four before ending their own lives. The day of the shootings, April 20, 1999, Rick and TJ (Tom Johnson), another friend and coworker, left campus to eat lunch. Ten minutes later the shootings began.

Because there was so much damage to the school, students and faculty shared a nearby school (Chatfield High School) while Columbine was being repaired.

Rick retired six years after the massacre at Columbine.

I did go to the funerals. I won't go to the memorials. As horrible as it sounds, once you work through five or six of them . . . TJ and I went to all of them together. You didn't feel like at the eighth, ninth, tenth, and eleventh that you were giving them [the dead] their just due. But you needed to be there. It was numbing to the point where you kind of think, *Jesus!* It was just overkill. It is a horrible way to put it but it was it was just all walks of life, different funerals, different ceremonies, different people. It was very different. I didn't have enough ties and suits.

When we went to Chatfield, I went the first two days, got the class squared away, and called in sick for two weeks. I said, *I'm not coming.* I wanted to be back in the building [Columbine] I didn't want to be at Chatfield. Chatfield had a planned fire drill

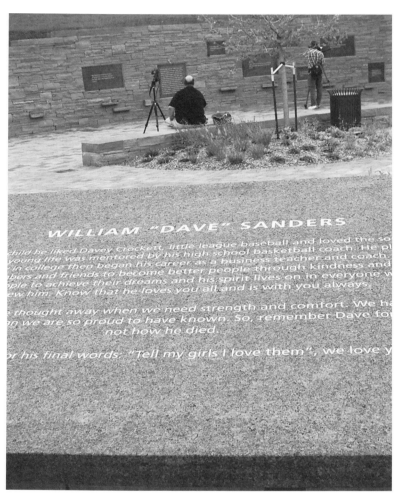

Memorial for Dave Sanders

Rick's friend Dave Sanders

and we were part of it. They announced that there was going to be a fire drill, we went outside, and I watched fifty teachers cry when the sirens went off because they had heard sirens for four or five hours when they were in Columbine. I hated it. I never went back into Chatfield again in the next six years.

Everybody at Chatfield exited their building at 12:30 or 1:30 every day. Everyone—custodians, cooks, administrators, teachers—every single person in the building was gone by 1:30 and every single person that worked at Columbine went in there. They busted their asses to do their jobs as good as they could, but for some reason that bothered me. I was glad to be back at Columbine. So I never went back to Chatfield, and I probably never will.

The next school year we went back [to Columbine] three or four days earlier like we always do, and then we were there for raising the flag and welcoming everyone back in. The first day back was real emotional for everyone. We were so enabling to the kids, so quick to meet their every need because we were so consumed about where they were psychologically. The staff was great at that, and the counselors were great at that, and the administrators were great at that, too, unless it was just really bad. I'm not sure we did them [the students] a favor. I'm not sure what else we would have done. I'm not sure if we were in that same situation if we would do anything different. But as the year went on what we did was we kind of created a freshman class that got away with stuff. But I don't know what [else] you would do. But that came at a cost, too, because the teachers and counselors and Frank [the principal] and the administrators—it cost you something emotionally and physically to do that for them when you're not doing stuff for yourself. Our counselors barely had their heads above water. We had all kinds of mental health options, and some people took advantage of it. I did and it was good. Some of those people continue to have problems.

There's just not any closure with anybody. You know the parents of the people that were killed and wounded, so many questions that are never going to be answered. I don't think they'd even be answered if [the killers'] parents would come forward and be totally honest with how they raised their kids and what they did. I'd like to know what they saw . . . but as far as parenting, you do the best job you can and it's still a wild card. I don't know how many teachers I've met that I thought were the most stand-up people I knew, did everything right. I thought they were stand-up individuals, married, and everything is great—and their kid is off-the-wall. You do what you can. It may be what they did. I'd like to know, but we're never going to know this. So somewhere down the line there needs to be some closure.

I'll have my moments for the school. I think about Dave [Sanders] a lot. Kids that were killed were in my class. One of them had just left my class and went to the library, Kelly Fleming. She left at passing period, same time as me and TJ. All she did was walk to the library, and TJ and I got in the car and went to 7-Eleven.

Everbody's watching this—[from] the SWAT team, to how Frank handles this—everything else that goes on is compared to Columbine High School. Sometimes I'm just driving down the road and thinking . . . I'm just astounded or bewildered, thinking, *I taught at Columbine High School and this happened.* It didn't happen at North High School. I'm not trying to put a spin on those guys but I'm *there*, cripes! It [was] such a good school—and it's still a good school—but it was such a good school and to take that kind of a hit. I'm sure other schools could have weathered that kind of storm, and other schools have, but it's a big hit.

When you're watching some of the movies that are out right now, you hear references to Columbine. I just would hate for that to be Columbine's legacy. I remember standing next to Mark Wilson, a reporter for the *Rocky Mountain News*, who graduated from Columbine, at the freshman orientation day and saying, "I just don't want this to be my legacy." That was a huge concern, that I didn't want that to be the only thing I remember about Columbine. It hurts that people that don't know what's going on, or associate gun violence and allegations of bullying with Columbine High School, and that bothers me a lot. It hurts. It hurt the first few years after it, when people . . . even some of my friends and acquaintances became so expert on what was wrong, but it didn't take long to set them straight. That hurts because they *don't* know. Just like the people who weren't there don't know. I feel an obligation to correct them. Other stuff, politics . . . but not this. This was too close and there is an obligation for me.

So many questions that are never going to be answered. I don't think they'd be answered even if [the killers'] parents would come forward and be totally honest with how they raised their kids and what they did.

We learned a lesson about the press. Oh God . . . and it was a tough lesson. We learned that no matter what they tell you, they are going to say whatever they want. They are going to take you out of context, they are going to come up with whatever they want to do, and they are going to go for their story. With the exception of one guy. A guy from ESPN did a story on Dave because Dave won the ESPY award in Las Vegas. The guys from ESPN came out, and he talked to everybody. He was a great guy. I sent him a Columbine jacket, and we still correspond occasionally. Unless Frank tells me to talk to them [reporters], I don't talk to them.

How did this impact my relationships? Well, TJ and I had been friends for God knows how long. We are just now starting to get back to where we were. A combination of whatever it was

Tom [TJ] and I are, the stress of whatever it was. He said some things to me, I said some things to him . . . we did this repeatedly probably a couple years after this whole thing happened. And finally I said, *Screw it. I'm done.* And that is just now starting to repair itself. That was a casualty.

How do I get through this? I work. It always has been [a coping mechanism]. I think you have to have a support group to deal with it. I think you need to get some counseling and talk through some things. I don't know if you *have* to go to counseling, but it seems like [you] can talk to [support] people about those things that you wouldn't talk to some other people about. I think I have even been mellower than when I was coaching and things pissed me off. I'm happy. I'm not happy about how things turned out. I wouldn't change much of anything except for that one moment. I don't want that to be my legacy, but I'm not going to dwell on that. There's too many good people out there . . . too many good kids, and they helped a lot, they really did.

Michelle Jeffries March 2005

Justice for Michelle meant having her eighteen-year-old son's killer behind bars. After four years of fighting the Seattle district attorney's office to ensure that her son's case would be taken seriously, she was left with a broken marriage and strained family relationships. It seemed to her that the pain in her heart would never go away. Even though she struggled daily with her destructive anger, she was determined to seek justice and mend the brokenness resulting from four years of hell.

Her son, William, was at a party with his older brother, Stephen. A fight broke out. The shooter went to his car, got a .40 caliber Glock, and came back to the party where he fatally shot William, who was unarmed. The shooter claimed self-defense, and the prosecutor's office dropped the case by reason of insufficient evidence.

That was a Saturday night—January 27, 2002. I get this phone call around 1:25 a.m. Stephen said, "I need you to come to the hospital. William's been shot!" So, *Oh my god, Oh my god!* I look outside and the snow is as twice as deep as it was before I went to bed. I thought, *How am I going to get this car through this steep hill? Okay, God, just let this be minimal; no death, maybe a missing arm, but not quadriplegic or nothing so severe that he wouldn't want to be alive.* And that is all I would concentrate on, that and how to get there faster. I thought, *Well maybe he is just going to lose an arm or leg.* I was starting to resolve within myself before I got

Michelle Jeffries

there, what it was going to be. Then I got there and Stephen and my other two kids were there. Everybody that's close to William was there before me. I kept thinking to myself, *Why is everybody here? How bad is this?* I said, "You tell me exactly what happened," and that's when he started telling me about how it evolved. My ears started ringing, and I don't know if I quite heard [it] all because my mind started going back to, *Okay, it's only a leg, it's only an arm.* Then the nurse came when he got midway through the story, and she said, "I have to give you the bad news that he's expired." I am thinking, *Expired into what and where? What do you mean? I want to know what are you talking about here.* My husband said, "Baby it is William, and William is dead." That is when I screamed and I said, "No, no, no, can't be him!" I kept saying, "No, no, no!"

The nurse said, "It is definitely him," and I hit the floor. I hit that floor and I couldn't breathe, and I asked God to move back. They took me outside because I couldn't get air. I just wanted to get to that room, and I begged them to let me go. "Maybe I can coax him to wake up. Let me get up and walk. I can do it." My husband just held onto me and wouldn't let me go back in there. Then they explained to me that he wasn't going to be comin' home. I said, "That's okay, we'll see him in the morning. I'll come back tomorrow." I didn't want to accept death. All the way home I thought, *Oh Lord he is quadriplegic. God, my baby's going to have no arms. . . .* My mind would not accept death.

I got home from the hospital [and] called my sister in Georgia. I said, "He's been shot but it's okay; he's gonna come home." She said, "No he's not comin' home to you, he's goin' home to Jesus." And that's when I understood. I would never get to talk to him, never get to hold him, never get to say I love you again. And I went numb for three years.

Michelle's sons William (left) and Stephen (right)

I didn't feel like I got to mourn. I went straight to angry because I never got a chance to say goodbye to my son because I was so busy fightin' [the prosecutor's office] and have continued to fight for justice. I couldn't even put William in the ground that day, mentally, because I knew I had to go find that prosecutor to make them give me some kind of paperwork. So there never was a goodbye. It made everything harder for me.

They said to me a week after he died, "Well you're not the wife, he wasn't married, he doesn't have any children, so you need to go through the Freedom of Information Act to get his records." I said, "What the hell is that? What does that mean?" They said, "Well, you need to go downtown. . . ." I said, "I'm not doing that. You're going to give me the paperwork. I deserve it!"

So we had a big long battle for a week and a half about me deserving the right for his paperwork because he lives under my roof. I supported him. He was only eighteen for six months before he was dead, so yeah, I want the papers.

A year and a half later, it was like, *Why won't the police release the information?* They held all this paperwork from me, and they wouldn't give me the autopsy report. I started digging into them and they go, "Oh, you're just a grieving mother, you don't comprehend what you are reading. It just depends on how you interpret it." The prosecutor said, "We can't see wasting the taxpayers' money. If you believe your son was shot in the back, go get us evidence."

I said, "So now you want me to do your job?" They know I don't have a lot of money and I work two jobs. I pay taxes and this boy did work. "Go spend *our* money on us!"

They [the city] put me through so much and it helped me what feels like murder my first son, Stevie, because I started doubting him. I started questioning him. I cried twenty-four hours a day. And this made it so bad between us. I didn't want to speak to him. At the time he was only twenty-nine and was telling me, "Mommy, I am telling you the truth." I placed William in Stevie's arms that night. "You are your brother's keeper. No, you didn't intend for this to happen but as a mother, how?" I got one in the ground and one above ground and I am so mad at . . . I don't even know who. I just have madness.

I see when I look at Stevie, that little-boy look in his eyes, *Mommy, I am so sorry. I didn't mean for this to happen.* I miss that relationship. I have lost both my sons. I walked around with a cold black heart for a long time. I was scared to love; scared to be loved 'cause I didn't feel like anyone should love me. My child is in the ground. Who am I to deserve anything? Why should Stevie deserve anything? These are the things that started going through my head.

I ran my husband off. That poor man. He couldn't take it anymore. The kids stopped comin' 'cause they knew I was crazy; I just didn't know it. How could I know? Then I started on him; he was the only thing left. The only one person that I really needed. I would say, "You never loved William. You always had a problem with him." I hurt so bad. Oh my pain! I didn't know what to do, how to do; I just did because it was required. I had to apologize to my husband because I was so deranged. I didn't know I was tearin' and destroying my own family . . . what was left. My whole pretense was on protecting them. How do you protect them then shoo them away?

I would never get to talk to him, never get to hold him, never get to say I love you again. And I went numb for three years.

I knew to wake up in the morning, and I knew to get into the shower, but I would just sit at that phone for nine hours a day trying to call people, get help. My husband would come home and say, "Baby, I—" I'd say, "Get out of my face, get away!" It was just attacking time. That was so mean. It was so bad, and I didn't realize I was doin' that. I had told my husband, "You just have to go. I'm tired of beatin' you up. I can't do this marriage. I did not marry you to hurt you. I didn't marry you to take you through all this pain and agony. I have to ask you to leave."

That's when the bitterness just got greater and greater. I couldn't stop it. How [do] I go to church and praise Jesus God Almighty, and then turn around and be nasty and mean to my own family—a part of Jesus and God? I felt one morning so bad about everything, I had to look back to make sure my brain hadn't oozed out on my pillow. It just felt like a big hole in the back of my head. Last May, that's when I started snapping back into reality. God just said, *That's enough. You've done enough damage.*

If it hadn't been for my grandchildren, I probably would have been way gone. I wanted to, as a mother, go kill that boy [who killed William], beat him from his toes and just get him. As a Christian, I prayed for him. *How do I not have these feelings? I am failing God, I'm failing my family, I'm failing myself. I failed William. I didn't protect him, and that was my job. I was the protector of all.* But I am not the protector of all, only God is.

I started looking in the Bible. I said, "There's nothin' in here about how a mother's supposed to feel." I was trying to find comfort. I want to love Stevie like I used to love him. And then I have to remember William over here. There's no describing the pain. I read the Bible. I got on my hands and knees. I cried and prayed and screamed and played music all day before I went to work. When I came in from work I rushed to just get on my hands and knees. I could hardly wait for those eight hours to go away so I could go and pray. *Why did all this have to happen and who was this lesson for?* But I still don't quite understand. Was this lesson for Stephen? Was it for William? Was it for me?

I've learned that I am not the person I thought I could be. I never knew I had such mean, spiteful hatred in me. I look at the relationships . . . even with my daughters. I started accusing them. "You guys know something you are not telling me. You are all siding against me. You're with the prosecutors, too." We had a memorial for William [two years after his death] and I openly said to them, "I apologize. I am so sorry. I believe everything."

Stevie didn't want to stay around me. I called him a murderer.

I called my own son a murderer. I had to get on my hands and knees for three days and purge myself. That's when I said to God, "You have to take me. I've done so much damage. I've been so unruly to you, to my family, to myself. You have to take me. I can't take this anymore."

I died with William; a lot of me died with William. If it hadn't been for my grandchildren—because my children were walkin' around on eggshells; they didn't know what to do for me. One day, my ten-year-old granddaughter called. "Grandma, are you still crying?" I said, "Well, yeah." She said, "Grandma, you have to stop crying so much. Uncle William's up in heaven. Don't you know he's got work to do?" I said, "Excuse me?" I was sitting there listening, but I wasn't really comprehending. "Don't you know he's got ten rooms to build, Grandma? Every time you cry he has to come from heaven and sit by you. That's stopping him from working. Grandma, don't cry like that anymore. I want my room in heaven."

It was just like God slapped me in my face. I thought, *Oh my god, what have I been doing? What have I been doing to my family? It's okay to do it to me but then to project it off onto them . . .*

Then my grandson came and he said to me, "Grandma, everything is always about Uncle William. Do you love us anymore?" I just looked at his little brown eyes, "I never stopped loving you. I'm so sorry I have mistreated everybody."

I thought, *You know what, you're going to mess up and miss your mark and never get to see him again. You will never get to wait in heaven for those who come.* I started really thinking, *How do I make amends? What do I do?*

I went out to the grave and I apologized to William for using him to make any excuse of why I treated my children so bad.

And I know he would never have wanted me to separate our family like this. I heard him tell me, "Mom, I'm okay. It's all right, I'm okay. Tell Stevie I'm all right." And then he left.

I had a close-knit, normal family. Life for me now is to live it as if everyday was the last day for sure. I never thought my child would go in a blink of an eye. I thought he would be here forever. I would be the grandmother—the great grandmother—going in the ground and everybody around me. But I don't know who's going to go first. It changed my whole optimism about what life really is. I thought it was in order, but there is no order. I will stay consumed until the judgment happens. I have also learned that I have to put it away sometimes and go and enjoy everybody else. It has changed my whole entire being. I'm not quite sure how it's changed, 'cause I have yet to walk the walk. I don't anticipate mapping it out. I know I need to plan this life, but I don't want to miss anything that my kids do.

Justice for me will have the murderer in custody for the rest of his life. And part of justice for William, that I know he would want me to do this: to eventually set up a scholarship fund for gifted children that want to draw or pursue drawing. Give somebody else the opportunity to grow.

I can smile because the pain was a buoy. Now it is a balloon. It is so much lighter. I still hurt. I still cry and ache. This part of the pain never goes away.

Jenny Wieland

The Friday before Thanksgiving of 1992, Jenny Wieland got the call that is every parent's worst nightmare. Her seventeen-year-old daughter Amy had gone to visit a friend and never returned to her suburban Seattle home. Jenny's only child was murdered when a teenaged boy, showing off his new gun, pointed it at the back of Amy's head and the gun went off. Amy died from that gunshot wound. At the time of this interview, fifteen years had passed since Amy's death.

Of course, back then I was living in a world where stuff like this didn't happen to middle-class people, especially out in the suburbs. I remember around five that morning when the doctor told us we needed to start thinking about donating organs. Because of the trauma to her brain she had suffered a heart attack, and they were unable to revive her. So I asked if I could see her. That was a surreal experience. She was lying on a table with a sheet covering her and she was already cold. She was my only child. I really thought my life was over. The next few days were really a blur.

I truly believed I wasn't going to survive it. At the time, I didn't know anybody who had experienced anything like that so there really was no one to talk to about that and the immediate aftermath. I [had been] living in that world with rose-colored glasses. I had talked to Amy about drugs and alcohol and birth control—all the things you talk to teenagers about. I had never talked to her about guns because it never entered my head that she would ever be around someone who had access to one.

Jenny Wieland

Jenny and her daughter Amy

I would wake up every day in tears. I didn't want to go on with life. Not suicidal thoughts, but just thoughts like: *How can anybody endure this pain? If something awful can happen to Amy, then what is left for the rest of our family? What can happen to me?*

I went through phases where I didn't want to leave the house. I would go to work but I got to thinking: *Well you know, someone can just shoot me on the freeway or something.* I had all kinds of intense fears.

He pled guilty to first-degree manslaughter, and he got the maximum sentence under Washington State law, but he actually only served twenty-seven months. When he got out it was total trauma again. Because he was from this area I kept thinking I could look over, driving to work on the freeway, and possibly see him. Or walk into a restaurant or into a movie theater, and what would I do? I still wonder today what I would do to or say to him.

It was so hard because she was murdered right around Thanksgiving time. I didn't want anything to do with Thanksgiving. I didn't want to be here in Washington State. In 1994 I bought a timeshare and started going to Mexico during the anniversary. I made sure I was there on the 20th and the 21st of November and then stayed through Thanksgiving. Then I could be in a country where I didn't have to celebrate Thanksgiving. Last year was actually the first year that I have actually cooked Thanksgiving dinner and had company. But it is still hard.

I didn't celebrate Christmas at all for five years. Then I started collecting angels and that is really how I began to acknowledge Christmas again. I just didn't want anything to do with it. I still wish in the beginning of October I could just go to sleep and wake up on January 1st.

There is something about every holiday that reminds me of Amy; even superficial holidays like Easter, Valentine's Day, and Halloween. There are all kinds of things that remind me of her. Since she was my only child and more and more of my friends are grandparents, I find that that has been difficult. I always think that as a parent there are all those rites of passage that you look forward to: high school graduation, college, getting married . . . All those things were taken away in an instant.

Your life completely changes when there has been a violent death. Every aspect of your life changes. A lot of the people you look to for support aren't there and that is hurtful. A lot of it has to do with that people aren't really educated about death and dying and really don't know what to say—so they don't say anything. Or what they do say is inappropriate. You suffer the loss of your loved one but then you suffer the loss of your support system. I would say that out of all my really close, close friends, I only have one that was a friend when Amy was still alive. To me that is astonishing.

When it happens, it undermines some really basic needs like the need to feel safe. The perpetrator—whether he is caught or not—makes you feel unsafe. If he's not caught, there is that fear that he is going to hurt someone else. You don't feel safe in your own world because you know that if something so horrible can happen to someone you love, then what's in it for you?

What is morbid for me is when someone comes in with a brand new baby. I hold it and look at it, and I always think, *I wonder if you are going to survive this world?*

The ability to trust changes. The fact that most victims know the perpetrator makes you have those guilt feeling like *If only this and only that*, so you lose the ability to trust people. Not only the ability to trust the people around you but in meeting new people. I also lost the ability to feel close to people. I did this for a long time. Even now, every time my fiancé leaves to go fishing I feel like there is this possibility that he is not coming back, 'cause Amy just left one day to go visit a friend and she never came back. People say, "Have a safe trip" and they say, "Oh, nothing is going to happen." Well I know that the worst can happen.

I can remember doing my victim's impact statement thinking, *How in the world can you explain to a judge how something like this happens in your life,* knowing that it had just happened so recently. So many times I wish I could go back and tell my story again. How it has changed since 1992, in every imaginable way.

I have learned that the things that once upset me seem so petty—the dishwasher breaks, having a washing machine overflow, getting stuck in traffic on I-5 . . . If that's the worst thing that happens to me today I am having a good day compared to someone else who found out that her loved one was shot and murdered.

What is morbid for me is when someone comes in with a brand new baby. I hold it and look at it, and I always think, *I wonder if you are going to survive this world?*

It's not so much regrets; it's always the what-ifs. I moved here from Spokane in 1986 because of Amy's dad. I was in a very bad domestic violence situation. Sometimes I think, *What if I hadn't moved? I might have been dead but Amy might have survived somehow.* I regret that I was a single parent for a long time. Because of that, and in order to provide Amy a good home, I feel like I missed out on certain aspects of her life.

At first I was really pissed at God. I thought, *If you do these good things, good things will happen.* So this happened and I thought, *But I have been a good person. How could this happen? How could God allow this to happen to such an innocent child?*

But then I went three hundred and sixty degrees and felt that it was only through God's strength that I was able to survive. What *doesn't* help is when the clergy will say stupid things like, "It was God's will," and "It was all in God's plan." People can get re-victimized by things like that.

I know for myself that at the time of Amy's death I was in

shock, and then in about six months it was all of a sudden so painful. I think peer support is really helpful where you can meet with others that have suffered similar losses. It validates your feelings and makes you feel like you are not going crazy. For the first few months after Amy's death, I felt like I was going crazy.

That first year a lot of the memories you think about, instead of making you happy, they make you sad. They aren't so comforting; they haunt. Then slowly but surely they get turned around and you think of your loved one and laugh, and then it is okay to laugh.

I am a pretty open griever, and I think that has been healthy for me—not to keep things bottled up. It is okay to be angry. Let it out. Just don't hurt yourself or others. People should find what works for them, like sitting at the computer, writing what you are going to do to the person who shot your loved one, printing it, and then throwing it in the garbage can. Go to a garage sale, get cheap china, and throw it inside the garage where they break. Or scream into a pillow. The reactions people are having are normal to a horribly abnormal event in their life.

Sudden violent deaths are so different in that the grief is different. There are no set stages of grief. They come and go and you can have something happen that takes you back to stage one whether it is a birthday, an anniversary, or the smell of cologne. Amy liked expensive cologne and I remember right after she was murdered I would smell that and I would just start crying. Or I would hear a song on the radio, same thing. That just takes you back to day one, and that can be unnerving. Eventually good days outnumber the bad days. You no longer have that pain that is so consuming that you can even feel it in your heart. It does subside.

I know that there is no timetable, and there is no right and wrong way to grieve. I would tell people that the most important thing is to take care of yourself. I have learned that the human spirit is indeed very strong in order to survive, especially in the case where a parent has had a child die. The fact that the human spirit *can* actually survive—that is amazing.

Cindy Johnson December 2006

Cindy and her fiancé, Steven, were expecting their first child together when he unexpectedly killed himself. After being together for only nine months, Cindy was left with two kids, Tyler (four) and Veronica (seven), from a previous relationship, and a newborn who would now be fatherless.

Every day at my lunch hour I would go get Veronica from school, and many times we would stop at a little convenience store. This day we stopped by the house. I heard our dog in the back kind of whining, crying in the backyard. I open up the back door and I notice that Steve's vehicle was in the back, and I was like, "Ohhh! Steve are you out here?" 'cause I thought he was maybe working on his car or something. He had the day off. So the dog is acting really weird and I'm like, "Steve are you back here?" I go back and open up the gate and I don't see him, and the dog again is freaking out and Veronica is running out to the back yard. "Steve, Steve!" I go over to the driver's side and the weird thing is that I noticed this thing sticking up by the steering wheel and I am like, *What is that?* As I got closer I realized it was the barrel of a gun. And I didn't see Steve but as soon as I got over to the driver's side I saw his body slumped over and a visual that nobody wants to experience. Bad dreams for many, many years, and they still appear. Definitely a visual that you do not want to see—ever.

I hear Veronica and everything is like a bad dream. I was just frozen. Time kind of stood still and I just yelled "STOP!"

Cindy Johnson and her daughter Dylan

Cindy and her fiancé Steve

And she's like, "What's wrong? Where's Steve?" And I'm like, "Go back in the house!" She obviously knew from the tone of my voice because Veronica was not a child that listened on the first time. She ran back into the house. It's weird 'cause I don't remember a lot. I called my best friend Janelle. She is like my sister. I don't remember that phone call, but apparently I told her what happened and that I needed her to pick up Tyler (my four-year-old) at daycare, and I don't remember what all happened. I was on survival mode. I don't remember a lot of stuff except for what Janelle has told me, like about giving birth to Dylan.

I went through all the stages [of grief] two years later. I was on survival mode for two years. It was just the weirdest thing. I don't remember quitting my job, I don't remember the move, I don't remember starting a job. It's just bizarre to me. So I started going to a support group, SBS [Suicide Bereavement Support]. I still go once in a while. It's always tough because I tend to relive everything. I don't want to go there but I know it's all part of healing, and I think it will always be a healing process.

I started to feel two years later. I never cried, and then about two years later it felt like when you are driving in a fog and then you just drive right out of it. Everything was just clear and that is when I started feeling it. I remember the day it happened. I lived in Long Beach, Washington. I don't even remember that. I married one of my best friends (Carl) that I grew up with, and he knew Steve really well. He loved Steve and he was devastated when it happened. He couldn't believe it happened. I think Carl's whole thing, because he was so close to Steve, was to take care of me. I think for me it was a sense of security. The weird thing is that I don't even remember the ceremony. I look back on pictures and I go, *Wow, crazy!* That ended up in disaster. They say when you go through a traumatic situation, don't make any big decisions or changes. I moved from Reno back to Washington, I changed jobs, I got married . . . I did everything I wasn't supposed to do. That led to divorce after two years. He said basically, *I can't compete with a ghost of Steve.* The fog cleared before this ended. Apparently that affected how the end result was.

Dylan is only twelve right now but we talk openly about it and I tell her to be open with her feelings about stuff. Veronica was real affected because she thought it was her fault. Every once in a while, out of the blue she'll go, "Mom, I wonder why he did that?" She'll say that one sentence. I wonder that, too. It didn't just affect me, it affected all three of us; it affected my best friend, it affected all of his family. It's endless. His other daughter, his friends, his coworkers, neighbors—it affected so many people.

We had everything to look forward to. We'd just bought the house on the river; we were remodeling. A week before, he had gone out and bought a swing set and set it up for Dylan and his kids, too. He was all excited. He was excited about a family reunion coming up in July, which I did go to when I was eight and a half months pregnant. I don't remember a lot of it.

Anniversaries? His birthday is January 7th and I always wish him a happy birthday. I have thought about doing a birthday cake, but it's a double-edged sword. Do you want to continue to bring that up or do you want to forget it? Every year, May 3rd [the day Steve died] . . . I have actually thought of trying to do something on a traditional basis because of Dylan. For me, I just want to forget it. It took me ten years to be able to put a picture up in the living room of Steve and to have pictures out. I have one up now and I have a photo album that Dylan can look through anytime. For a long time they were packed away.

A lot of people don't understand. I understand that people experience all kinds of hell in their life. It's all so personal. They don't understand the callus inside that I have because of this. I felt the ultimate rejection. They say, "Don't take it personally." I have seen counselors and support groups who say, *You can't take it personally; this was Steve's issue* . . . but you can't help it. Just like Dylan. Dylan thinks, *Did he not want me? Was it my fault?* All that . . . It may not evolve, process through her, but I'm thinking some of it has. But that anger, that guilt, that wonder, that question that will always be open-ended. It has totally affected my trust with other people. One thing you kinda say, *You know, nothing can ever hurt me as bad as that hurt me.* But then again, that's a guard and a callus, which don't let people all the way in either, and that's a problem. On one side you go, *Wow, people I love, I want to make sure they know that every day because I never want them to doubt that.* It's a double-edged sword. You can almost smother people to death because you want them to know they are important but on the other hand . . . it's a weird experience to live with.

Through the years I have had a couple different gunfire experiences. At seven years old my dog got into my brothers guinea pig cage and killed his guinea pig. My brother was mad. He took my dog out to the backyard, right in front of me, and shot my dog. I remember that vividly. It was devastating to me. At that point I thought, *Wow guns are* . . . He was in a rage. If he had not been in an emotional state, he would never have done that. He is a very cool and collected guy, but he was in a rage. He's five years older than I am. That was my first bad gun experience.

The second one was when I was nineteen. I was a graveyard waitress in California. It was a rough city, Oakland. We had a large group that came in from the Coliseum after the Raiders played. They had been drinking. A lady was very irritated at me. Apparently we had put butter on her pancakes. Anyway, so she took it out on me and was threatening to kill me. They escorted her out and when she left she was like, "I'll be back!" She did come back and had a gun in her bag and pointed it right at me and our security guard tackled her.

She was drunk and angry. The situation with Steve putting a rifle to his head . . . I hate guns. I'm very careful if the kids go over to a friend's house. I ask, "Do they have guns?" I don't ever want to see or touch a gun—ever. I didn't let the kids ever play with toy guns. I just don't like them.

This has affected me with trust issues; fear of getting close to anybody, fear of safety for my children and myself. The gun control is out of control in our world. I understand that the NRA just hate when people talk bad about guns. Maybe they haven't experienced what some people have. If you have not been in those pair of shoes then . . . I know there is training and the kids go hunting. I understand that, but there is a whole other side of that. It's changed my world completely in so many ways. I think any bad experience, any traumatic experience, it defines you. There's no way it can't. I'm a really strong person and I'm really a survivor and I really believe I am moving forward, but you can't do anything but look at the past.

It is an embarrassing thing. With a murder, there is a lot of empathy from others. Suicide, you are looked at kind of like, *Oh my god!* almost like damaged goods.

Steve and I had, from the beginning, always surprised each other with little gifts and notes. The short time he lived, I experienced more in a relationship than some people do in twenty years in terms of the quality. I feel very fortunate that I got to experience that love and that unconditional love and caring for someone. My heart is looking for that again but my mind ain't there. I think that's a problem with a lot of relationships. I don't know if I am capable of giving all that and letting my guard down, and letting someone in.

One thing I am grateful for is that, with the mental state that he was in, which I can't even relate to, I am so appreciative that he didn't take me, Veronica, and Tyler with him. That's the only grateful thing I got out of this whole thing. Because when that happens, we hear about it every day: murder/suicide. Not that I would ever think he would do that but I never thought he would commit suicide, so what kind of mental state was he in?

It is an embarrassing thing. With a murder, there is a lot of empathy from others. Suicide, you are looked at kind of like, *Oh my god!* almost like damaged goods. I'm thinking there is something majorly wrong with me. But then it's not my fault,

I shouldn't feel guilty; it's nothing I did or didn't do. You totally go there, *What did I do? What didn't I do? What should I have done? . . . Should I have seen that?* You go over and over like a broken record. You have all this to deal with. I still have this dream where he appears. I'm in our bedroom in our Reno house, he appears at the door just like how I saw him last, when I found him, but he is standing up and he is alive. It's the worst horror movie you would ever want to see.

I don't think it will ever *not* be painful. I reach for that but I know realistically that it will always be painful. One thing that makes me not want to tell people what happened is because of people thinking, *Wow, he didn't want to be with you that bad that he put a gun to his head?* I worry about people thinking that. *My god, what's wrong with you?*

I've pretty much raised the kids mostly on my own the last twelve years, and I think I've done a hell of a job. They are responsible kids. They are great kids—well-mannered, hard workers, no trouble, good students. And I think it's important to laugh a lot. We do laugh a lot. We are very silly. I see Steve in Dylan's face. It's her eyes. She has my shape of face but his eyes . . . I love that about her. Sometimes it's like looking at a ghost and it's just like, *Wow!* She is my little angel.

I am still struggling and I probably always will. At this point I just try and surround myself with as much positive as possible. That is really important. My kids are a huge positive in my life and my job, [which] I love, and it's a huge positive. It's very important to do what you like to do. The reason I think I work so much is to stay busy. I am a very busy person, and I know that the reason I stay busy so much is so that I don't have to stop and think about it. So it's almost a denial thing, which is a bad thing, but that is my way of dealing—by keeping busy.

Sandie Williamson June 2007

Sandie's only child, Christopher, was twenty-one years old when he was shot multiple times by a lonely, deranged twenty-eight-year-old that he and his fellow ravers had invited into their close-knit group. On March 25, 2006, at 7 a.m., Kyle Huff, after three months of planning, shot and killed six and injured three, all in their late teens and early twenties, before killing himself at a rave after-party in Seattle. It was Seattle's worst mass murder in over twenty years. Sandie continues the daily struggle to move forward without her son, with heavy regret that she never knew or appreciated how kind and helpful he was to all who met him.

I was almost thirty-nine when Chris was born. He was my miracle baby. He was always a good baby; the one thing I didn't know about Chris was that he was a wonderful *son*. He kept his other life pretty separate from ours. He'd be on the computer and I'd say, "Chris go make some friends. Get off that computer!" He had tons of friends; there were over five hundred people at the memorial. He had hundreds of friends, but I didn't know it. He'd go up to Capitol Hill [where] he'd feed the homeless kids. He would try to get them places to live. He gave them his clothes, and this whole time I'm saying, "Go make friends, go make friends!"

One [time] he spent four days gone. It was not my happiest time with him. He did not call. I did not find out [he was

Sandie Williamson

Sandie and her son Christopher

helping others] because Chris never told me the nice things he was doing. He was never one to, you know. . . . He just let me rag on him when he got home. He had been helping this fifteen-year-old girl. Her stepfather had been molesting her for years. The mother was afraid to do anything, so Chris and her spent four nights under the Aurora Bridge. Every morning he would take her to the different agencies trying to get her help. And finally after the fourth day—she talked to me at the memorial—she had said to him, "I don't want you to think I've given up on you, but I'm hungry and I'm tired and anything's better than sleeping under a bridge." He stayed awake the whole time to keep her safe.

He really loved music. He was really getting into it, and that's why he was there that night, to play a little. He worked at Fred Meyer and went to school at North Seattle Community College, and Friday nights he went to the raves. But he was getting out of it. He was done. He says, "It's time for me to grow up." It was on his MySpace [Web page], "I feel like if I don't, I never will." Usually [at] the raves, the kids are from fourteen to twenty-one, and then you usually move up to the twenty-one drinking. That wasn't his scene. So this was his last one, his last rave.

The people that were really close to him were just devastated. Several kids have killed themselves since the shooting. That was pretty soon thereafter. I go on there and read the blogs and bulletins, and a lot of the kids have stopped going to the raves. The whole thing took away their trust. Their whole thing was just loving each other, trusting each other; and that trust was destroyed. Their little world that they tried to keep happy and safe, this person . . . the one thing they stood for was inviting everybody into their world, and they all feel responsible to a degree. If they hadn't been so loving maybe Chris would be alive today. It's just different. They don't have that trust.

Oh, the first six months—I waited. Four o'clock every morning, I'd wake up because if there was a rave that's about the time he got home. So I'd just wake up. "Oh my god, that was a terrible dream I just had!" I actually thought that what happened was a dream. I'd run downstairs and I didn't see Chris. So for along time I thought it was a dream. You know you'd wake up and go, *phew!* I just wanted to go down and hug him and promise him that I'd never yell at him again and I was never going to give him heck for not coming home. I'm not saying he was perfect. I mean, he caused me anguish but he was out helping people.

There must have been a hundred people that got up and told stories about Chris [at his funeral]. Wonderful stories. This one guy was saying how he'd been down at the fountain at the Seattle Center, and he was going to kill himself. Then Chris came be-boppin' up. He said, "This guy [Chris] was so happy, it kind of disgusted me. I mean, I was really miserable and Chris said something like, *How's it goin'?*" And the guy said, "Not very well. You just better move over 'cause I'm going to kill myself. I have nothing, my girlfriend dumped me . . ." and Chris goes, "Oh that's cool, go ahead and do what you gotta do." And the guy said, "Well you don't have to be right here." And Chris goes, "Well how are ya going to do it?" "I have a knife." And Chris goes, "I collect knives, can I see it?" And the guy pulls out this big knife and he goes, "Can I see it just before you do it?" And the guy hands it to him and Chris immediately pops the blade off and the guy popped him and knocked him backwards and knocked out two of Christopher's teeth. And he says, "If you get up I'll hit you again!" And Christopher goes, "Fine, 'cause I'm not leaving you till we get you help." They were together I guess three more days until this guy got over it, got the help he needed.

What makes me feel better? Nothing . . . my girlfriend, Terry. She's a counselor and she feels my pain. I know she feels my pain; she's got three children, and she loved Chris. Chris used to babysit her kids. I babysat her kids—that's how I met her. Talking to her, I don't know, she just says the right words. She's had brain cancer and thyroid cancer and she says, "I'd go through all that but I could never go through what you're going through." She loved Chris. He would go over there and work in her yard and babysit her kids. He was so kind and everybody loved him and now he's gone.

I go down into his room and I smell his bed. I've never turned off his bedroom light. I haven't touched anything. I didn't think it was possible to love somebody so much. I know you love your kids but maybe it was 'cause I was an older mom and all I thought about was him 'cause I already had everything. Maybe 'cause he was so kind. I spray his cologne and smell his room. His cat sleeps down here.

I would lay in bed and hear his voice for months 'cause he would always come in and go, "Hi, Mom." And I would hear that and I would think there had been a mistake. I couldn't view his body. He had an open casket but I couldn't look at him. I didn't want to be able to visualize him that way. Because that is what I would visualize and that is what I would see. Now I can see him coming home with no hoodie on, just a t-shirt on going, "Hi, Mom." He never just walked in, it was always, "Hi, Mom." Half the time I'd tear into him and he just let me. He didn't say he was helping people. He just let me, and I'm having a hard time with that. I'd give anything if he never called or if he didn't come home for six days. I wouldn't say anything if I just had him back—I don't think he knew I loved him.

I used to be spiritual. I used to be a deacon in a church. I've been to a church once since. A couple of weeks later [after his death] I walked into the church and the first song they were singing was "God Will Protect You." I started crying 'cause it was a lie; he couldn't protect him. There was no reason for those kids to be killed. They weren't doing drugs, they didn't have weapons, they weren't drinking and driving. All the things you teach them not to do, they never did them. There's no reason. So where was God? Why didn't he protect Chris? Why didn't he have Kyle Huff get a flat tire, or his car wouldn't start, or his lock jammed, or his gun jammed? Where was our God? I want to . . . I want so much to believe I'll see him again. Even the minister from our church is lost. He stayed for a year and then things got worse. He said he questioned things. How could such a wonderful young man that never hurt anyone, never cursed, drink, do drugs, was respectful to everyone . . . ? You can ask anyone. You'd think I'd ordered him out of a catalog. Not that he didn't do some things. In high school he went from straight As to flunking, but overall, for a twenty-one-year-old man . . . He would have been a wonderful husband.

He was my success story. He was me—all my hard work and going without vacations and everything he was. And he was going to carry on my legacy. He was going to have me twelve grandbabies. He said we were going to live here and all I had to do was play with the kids because I'd been in daycare for forty-three years. I love kids and I wanted to have grandbabies. I wanted to have a daughter-in-law not to like. I don't have those things. He [Kyle Huff] didn't kill just Chris—he killed my future.

I don't think he knew I loved him.

But my girlfriend, she's . . . I will tell you that if it had not been for Terry, I would have killed myself a long time ago. I wanted to be with Chris so bad. I didn't care and if I couldn't be with him, then I didn't want to be here without him. I'm still here because I have an aunt that's eighty-seven, and I have to take care of her. I can't go anywhere until she's taken care of. I can't leave her 'cause nobody else will take care of her. The other night I told Terry, I said, "I don't know, it just feels like it's time to go." And she gives me the what for, and "Don't you think of it! I need you. Who's going to listen to me about my wacky kids?" 'Cause if she needs me, I can't do that to her. It's not like I hate life, it's quite the contrary. I feel like I have so much—except for the one thing that I need. I have three houses. I would give them all away to have Chris, I swear to God. It's not really important if you don't have someone to share it with. I totally would. And I worked so hard.

When I see news about other shootings, it takes me right back. About a month or so after, there was a shooting downtown at the Jewish Center. I sat there and I almost passed out. I was at my aunt's house, I started hysterically crying and it was just like . . . it brings it all up again. Every time. I can feel those parents' pain. Even if they're gang members, that mom isn't a gang member. Her son's not coming home. Her pain is the same as my pain. We do the best we can do, but why?

I lost my uncle. My aunt and uncle kinda raised me, and I loved him so much. He was just the greatest man. When he died I thought my world was over, but you know, it's a different kind of feeling and it wasn't as intense. It was a lot of loneliness. This isn't loneliness. See, I'm not lonely because Chris is gone; I *hurt* because Chris is gone. I was lonely because my uncle, he got me into gardening. We couldn't talk about our values anymore. We couldn't watch our western movies anymore. I'm not lonely. I hurt. I have a pain in my stomach all the time. I'm taking stomach medicine. At first I lost twenty-two pounds, and now I've gained it back. I'm not crying like I was. I cried 24/7 for months and months. I'm not crying like that. I didn't work for six months. I couldn't be around the kids. I went back to work. That helps me, being around the children that I love. I still miss him so much that I can't believe it.

I don't belong anywhere. I went to Friends & Families of Violent Crimes but when I went there, there were three other people. One lost his sister fifteen years ago; another was nine [years earlier]. We weren't on the same page. They were talking like, "Yeah they found her dead by the train. Her guts were pouring out . . ." Plus the way I feel, unless they can bring him back, what good are they going to do me? "I'm so sorry, Sandie, I know your pain . . ." but that's not going to make me feel better. I've read lots of books and I'm going through all the steps. I realize that, no, I'm not going crazy and that this could go on for years—the way I feel.

I have met with the other families [whose children were killed at the rave] but their lives are a little fuller than mine; like one of them has a grandbaby now and [they] have other kids and husbands. Whenever we have a gathering, even from the start, they don't seem as upset as I feel. I am a strong woman but not when it came to Chris. So they're not sitting there, waiting for their children to come home. He always kissed me goodbye in front of his friends, and he always called me "Pretty Mama." I asked him if he minded having an older mom, and he goes, "No, you're beautiful." And so he would always kiss me and say, Goodbye Pretty Mama"—that morning he did.

I know that if my faith was stronger I would have my Christian family. If you have faith then you know that he's in heaven; you know you're going to see him again. You know this. I really thought that I had worked really hard the last eight years—I joined the church and everything—that I was getting to that point. But see, then I realized that I doubted it right away. See, otherwise I'd be all right if I knew Chris was all right.

He was my best friend. A twenty-one-year-old son was my best friend, but he was the one person I knew that wouldn't lie, wouldn't steal, wouldn't hurt me, wouldn't call me names, wouldn't get angry to the point where I'd feel like a knife going in me. That never happened. I ragged at him. I'll admit it. But see, my worst fear happened.

Another human being took his life. People get cancer and people . . . those are things you can't prevent or couldn't have been prevented. Those things happen, or strokes or a plane going down, but this guy, point blank from you to me, shot him. Looked him in the face and shot him repeatedly, over and over. I mean how can you do that to anybody? It's broad daylight. It's not at night. Can you pull out a gun right now after talking to me and do that? I mean how can you do that? He talked to him for two and a half hours. He knew this young man; he knew my son and Chris would never have said something to upset him. He was talking to him about music and if anything he'd say, *Get out of my way. I can't shoot you; I know you. I can't do this, you were kind to me in there.* Christopher's kindness got him killed. He should have ignored this guy, gone back and talked to the rest of the kids. Because he got involved, because he helped people . . . he held him while the other kids got out the back of the house as he [Kyle Huff] shot his [Chris's] leg off, blew out the back of his head, and then shot him a fourth time when he was already dead. He butchered him when he didn't need to. He was dying from the first shot in the chest. He was dying. They were this close.

Twenty minutes after dropping off her eleven-year-old daughter, Haley, down the street with some friends, Kari came home to a devastating scene. Her husband of fifteen years, Tracey, had lain down on their bed, placed his shotgun to his head, and ended his life. As she struggled with her pain and over-whelming sadness, her job as a mother continued. She focused on helping her daughter deal with the loss of her father. Two years later she was diagnosed with breast cancer and opted to have both breasts removed in an attempt to ensure that her daughter would not have to experience the death of her one remaining parent.

Part I

I walked into the door. He had actually used a shotgun, and he had shot himself in the head. Horrible, horrible sight. It's not even like they show on TV. On TV they show a little bullet hole and a little blood running out, and it wasn't like that at all. His whole face was gone, the top of his head was gone, and his eyes were hanging out of their sockets. It was just so much blood. The whole wall was just red all the way up to the ceiling. It was like somebody had thrown paint and splattered everywhere. The rest of him was just normal, just lying there. The first thing I saw when I walked in was the wall; I was looking at the wall like, *What the hell happened to the wall?* Like my mind couldn't register what my eyes were seeing.

Kari Oswold and her daughter Haley

Kari and Tracey with their daughter Haley

It was a shotgun, so he had to use a paint stick to get the trigger because the barrel was so long. He was just lying on the bed like you would go to sleep. I didn't go to him. There was no chance he was alive. I knew he was gone. I just stood in the doorway, and then I ran downstairs and I was thinking, *I don't know what to do.* I ran outside.

When I look back now I realize he was depressed, but at the time I didn't know what depression was. I feel like it was a spur-of-the-moment decision. His blood alcohol came back at .24 and .26, three times the legal limit. I think because he had been struggling [with alcoholism] for so many months that, what I understand now, he was depressed about it. Maybe he wouldn't share because he was a guy; didn't say, *I feel bad today.* He didn't say anything like that, but I was on him. I was mad at him. I was frustrated, and I was thinking that he was going to come to me any day and say, *It's time for me to go back to treatment.* I was just waiting for that. I was hard on him because I was just so tired of it.

I didn't call to Haley right away. She was then an hour away at another friend's home. I was trying to figure out, *What am I going to do, what am I going to do?* Tracey's dad was of the opinion, "We don't tell her. Just say that he died." I know from the second it happened that I wouldn't do that; that I would be truthful because, first of all, forty-year-old men don't just die. Nobody's going to believe that. If the family knows, how are you ever going to prevent one person from not slipping? I'm not about that. I've never been about that. I knew right away that I would tell her the truth.

We drove up to Bellingham; it was so late, eleven o'clock. He died at about four-thirty. I had called my friends and told them what had happened and that we would come up but not to say anything to her. I didn't want somebody else telling her. When I got up there she was just watching a movie with her friend. The parents pulled her friend out of the room, and I explained to her that her dad had died, and I explained that it was with a gun—he took his own life. I didn't know anything about suicide. I never even knew anybody. At that moment that was all she could take in. She was in shock too.

She cried a little bit but she couldn't grasp it. What I noticed about her was that the next day she asked me a few more questions, like she would say, "Tell me again what happened?" But over the course of about two years each time she would ask, I would give her only as much information as she had asked. I remember so specifically, it was a couple of weeks after . . . she asked me to tell her the story that I had told her before; it was about how I found him. "He was lying down." A couple of weeks later she said, "Did he bleed?" So her little mind started processing it. When she asked that, I said, "Yes he bled." That was kind-of all she wanted to hear. Then a few months later she would ask me to tell her the story again. When we would get to the part where I said he bled, "Well how much did he bleed?" A few months later it was, "Where did he shoot himself?" Every time it was a little more until she got all the details. She kind of regulated herself. She knew she could only take in so much of the details, and then she would stop and move to a different topic. I wanted to tell her the truth. I never *didn't* tell her the truth. I kind of knew enough to respect her age and to know: a little bit at a time. I answered only her questions.

The whole upstairs . . . the room had to be completely torn apart, because of all the blood. They took everything. They took my nightstand, my lamp, my clock radio, the bedding and the carpet. The walls they scraped that night. Haley never saw it.

She never saw any of it—the icky stuff. She never saw it broken down to nothing. I had a priest come before we came back and blessed the room and blessed the house. But to her, she was not part of that violence scene. Luckily, this house didn't mean anything bad to her. It meant her Dad, her family. It was everything good to her. I think a lot of people would have moved out. It happened in the bedroom in the house but I couldn't move out because this was her stability. This was everything she loved. She was so happy here—all her friends right in the same neighborhood, her school within walking distance. I had to take sleeping pills to stay in that room.

You can't stop some thug from doing something to you. You can't prevent a suicide. You just don't have the control.

I tried to do a bunch of research on children and how violence affects them, because I wanted to know what to do for her. As a mother, how do I make this okay for her? I had the issue of the suicide, where I had to understand and help her to understand that it wasn't that he didn't love her or that he wanted something bad to happen to our family: it was that he was sick. There was something broken in his brain, and it couldn't think right. It couldn't make good decisions, and he didn't know to tell people because it was broken.

I had to dispel the suicide part; that put it into perspective for her. A person dies of suicide. I don't believe they commit suicide. I believe it was an illness just like cancer or like leukemia where they don't choose to be sick in the head. Nobody chooses to have cancer. It happens, and I couldn't prevent it. I couldn't stop it from happening to Tracey.

What I learned from my grief counselor was that adults take in the pain all at once. That is why adults fall apart. They fall down, they can't work, they can't think. Because it is so over-whelming, coming in all at the same time. *My husband died of suicide. He hurt himself. His pretty face is gone.* I was thinking, *I'm alone. I'm scared. I have to support my family. I have to raise our little daughter and I don't know how to teach her some of the manly stuff. I'm such a girly girl. I'm a widow at forty, and I had this whole life planned out. I have to do it myself. I don't even know where my investment papers are. I have to work and how do I get home in time to take care of Haley, because he was always home.* All these things, all at once, are on your shoulders. And a little kid . . . they hear that their father had died and they cry and then the next day they say, "Can I go play?"

The kids just take in a little bit at a time. Like today they realize, *Oh, my Dad isn't here to take me to school.* They don't understand, *Oh my Dad won't be here when I get married, and my Dad won't hold my child when its born, and my Dad won't help me move into my college dorm room.* They don't think of all that stuff.

I let her see me cry, but I didn't fall apart. I don't know if I can explain the difference. It was like I never hid that I was crying or sad, but I also didn't stop going to her basketball games. I didn't stop going to work. I didn't stop living a normal life because of the grief. I didn't want her to think that everything was about our grief. I tried to help teach her, too, that this one horrendous, hideous thing happened to us, but we have thousands of great things in our life. We have this fabulous family, all these cousins, we have basketball games, we have great grades at school, and we are so lucky.

Then you also try and use it as a teaching tool for your kid, especially a daughter. I keep talking to her about the positive. We know we can make it through this, and we can have a really good life, have lots of fun. We have all of our friends around us. Not a single friend left us, not a single family member. Everybody just came to our rescue despite the weird circumstances. If we can get through things like this . . . Heck, what does it matter if a boyfriend dumps you? What does it matter if something doesn't work out at the job? It's like those are so minor compared to what we have already experienced and know we can get through. Maybe if I can show her the positive ways to handle this when she gets old, she won't be one of those adults that flies into a hole every time something happens that isn't really that disastrous.

We really had to work through both of us being embarrassed that he died by a gun to his head. That's just not normal in suburbia. That's not what your friends have experienced. So I had to work really hard to not be embarrassed by it. That is why I think I spent so much time learning about it, because I wanted to understand what the hell happened. How does this happen in a normal house, in a man that has so much? How does he make that decision one day, and why a gun? Why not some nice pills or something where you just go to sleep?

Haley and I have gotten good at being on our own. We figured out that we can do it. Things break. . . . He was also like "Tim the Tool Man." He was just one of those kind of guys that if any thing looked like it was about to break, he was fixing it. I didn't even know how to change a lightbulb—in all seriousness. When these light bulbs started going out I was like, "I wonder how you get them down?" I never took care of anything, anything around the house. I mowed the grass once in our whole fifteen years of marriage, and that was because he was gone for three weeks

Kari and her husband Tracey

and somebody had to do it. I just didn't do any of that stuff. So I think we spent three years getting used to it going, "Okay, we can do this." I hire out the gardening. I hire help when something breaks. I can do this."

At a young age there just really aren't that many people who've lost a husband or lost a child. We're young for that. People assume I'm divorced, and I don't like that either because I don't want them to think I'm divorced. There is a stigma around that. I'm not divorced. I love my husband and he should be here. When you say, "My husband passed away," they say, "What happened?" I would ask the same way. I never knew that. And then when you respond, "It was suicide." Their face goes white. They stammer all over the place. They don't know what to do. You want to give them two books' worth of information 'cause a sentence isn't enough.

I role-played with Haley on how to respond to that because at her age—what does a kid say? Obviously, a kid is going to say, *What happened to your dad?* Or, *Where is your dad?* Or, *Why doesn't your dad live here?* So I role-played and role-played with her. "How are you going to answer that?" She was not capable of answering that.

At first when they asked me, I stammered all over the place, and then I got my verbiage down. The people who know—my friends, my family—I am very open with them. They know every detail they want to know. I'm very open. To my acquaintances who ask, I say, "It's very personal and I don't like to talk about it," 'cause it's like, I don't *have* to talk about it. It hurt me in the beginning. I was trying to explain to them and it was like, *Why am I telling this person? I don't even want to tell them this.* But for both me and Haley, we had to learn how to say what we wanted to say and who we wanted to say it to.

I truly don't think in a death like this that you'll heal. You'll get past it, but you don't ever get to leave it behind. It is part of who you are. It's a pain. I think you gain control of it and it softens; the edge softens. It is such a deep pain. You never get to put it behind you.

Part 2

You get to a point where that first year all you can focus on is, *How could this happen? How could he have felt this way? How could he have used a gun in that way?* I just missed him. He was a part of my life for twenty years. The second year, you're just sad because you realize all your thinking isn't changing anything. It's not figuring anything out. You don't get any answers. I think with any gun death there are not good answers because something wrong happened. Somebody made a bad decision and used it [a gun] for a bad purpose. I think anybody who has experienced gun violence spends so much time trying to make sense of it, trying to put it into a box that you can handle. You can't get those answers. You can't stop some thug from doing something to you. You can't prevent a suicide. You just don't have the control. That part, to me, was the most overwhelming—not being able to get an answer that makes sense. So the second year, you are so sad because you are realizing you're not going to get answers no matter how hard you try and figure it out.

I prayed and prayed and prayed, and finally I just started praying for peace. Somehow I just accept that it happened on this earth, and I don't get to understand what went wrong or what I should have done differently. I just didn't have the insight. I don't know now if I would figure it out even knowing what I know now.

Then when this hit [breast cancer], *Oh no, who is going to take care of me, what do I do now?* And I'm a proud person, too. I don't like to bother others . . . I don't want somebody to think they have to take care of me. It's different because it's back to the same thing as when Tracey died. I didn't want to bother Haley with the weight of it. She's a kid. And now she is fifteen. She's still a kid. She can't be responsible for me, yet things aren't the same. I'm tired. I had to go through the surgery and started the chemo at the end of December, and it's a really hard feeling, knowing he's not here to help. He would be driving me to my appointments. He would be making dinner. He would make it so easy, and I can't have that and it makes me miss him so.

I didn't have to have the double mastectomy. They said I really probably needed to only have it on the left side because of the way the cancer had spread. It was invasive enough in my breast tissue that if I had a lumpectomy they might not be able to get it all out and then they might have to [go] back and do the mastectomy. I would be left with so little that I would kind of be a mess. So that was pretty easy to do the mastectomy, but then when I thought about the recurrence on the other side, being a single parent . . . I can't do this; I cannot have any chance of not doing everything I possibly can. It turned out for me there was cancer on the other side; they just couldn't detect it because it was so early. Thank God I made the right decision on that end. That was done.

Some women say they don't want to do chemotherapy. I was like, *I can't not do it. I have to do every single thing possible, not just for myself—I don't want it back again—but for her* [Haley]. *I cannot be gone. I cannot risk doing anything else that would harm her.* It even broke my heart to tell her that I had cancer, even though I think my prognosis is excellent based on everything I am doing. It's really excellent. So at least I could tell her that. But I hated even to tell her that because of everything she had been through with her dad. I didn't want her to worry about me.

To reach out and touch someone who has been through it; I think that way about this cancer thing. The things that have helped me the most are talking to other women who have had the same surgery, who have had the same chemo. Knowing what to expect or how they coped with it, that you might emulate it. I think it's the same way with a tragic death—that is if you can find somebody. I've been meaning to go up to our church. It's time for me to give back and to say to the priest, *If somebody in our community dies of suicide, contact me. Let me talk to that person so they at least know they are not some leper in the community and they don't have to hide and be so embarrassed by it.*

Tasha Ross

March 2003

*Raising two teen boys in a rough Denver neighbor-
hood where gunshots and ambulance sirens are part
of the nightly routine was difficult for forty-five-
year-old Tasha Ross. When you leave for work at
three o'clock in the morning, it's tough to always know
where your kids are and what they're doing. Tasha's
seventeen-year-old son, Lamont, had spent time in
jail, but Tasha was proud of his kindness to other
kids in the neighborhood, and that he'd never hurt
anyone. But in such neighborhoods death is never far
away. Lamont was murdered because of something
that happened at a party he didn't even attend.*

*During a spring break party in 2001 someone
stepped on Edward Brown's foot. He responded by
firing a shot into the air, a shot that killed fourteen-
year-old Felix Sharp. In the days after the party,
Brown made a list of people who'd talked to the police
investigating Sharp's death. At a graduation party
two months later, Brown shot and killed a friend of
Lamont Ross who was on "the list." Lamont was
stunned and angered by the death of his friend. He
got a gun and went looking for Edward Brown. He
never used it. The next day Brown hunted Lamont
Ross down and shot him dead as he sat in his car.*

*Today, after two painful and drawn-out trials,
Brown and his accomplice, Joshua Swan, are in pris-
on serving a life sentence without parole. But Tasha
Ross is also in a prison of sorts.*

130 · Beyond the Bullet

Tasha Ross

Tasha with her sons Lamont (left) and LonEal (right)

He [Lamont] got in a lot of trouble. He got in trouble at school; he got in trouble on the streets. But he has never been in trouble for hurting another human being. He did the basic things boys do at school—skipping school. He even had to do time at an Arapahoe detention center because his probation officer said, "You're a good kid. You come from a good home. Why are you doing these things? I'm going to put you in, lock you up for two weeks to see how you like it." He was trying to show him a lesson. That worked for a minute. He got out, got a year older. He figured, *Okay, I'm going to do this, I'm going to do that.* Ended up doing a year in Lookout Mountain for teenagers. He has never been in trouble for hurting another human being.

Your kids get to a certain age—I don't care what nobody says. We all raise our kids up to respect adults and to be right, not do drugs, not do this and that. But when they get a certain age and they're eighteen and you tell them, "You can't go by my rules? Don't come home." Okay: *My mama's got to go to work at three o'clock in the morning . . .* and I gotta go to sleep. You can tell they'd been in and out. Everybody's kids might not be like that, but that's how it was for them. They was able to come and go because of the hours I worked. But just to wake up and see them in their bed asleep would be a grace to me. I'd say, *Thank you, Jesus; that's not my son out there hurt.* My heart goes out to whoever's child it was—don't get me wrong—but it was a feeling to walk in and know your child was in there sleeping peaceful. Just to know your kids is downstairs or in the front yard and you see the sirens or hear about something, and you can say, *My child is right here.*

I felt like I was the only person in this world who lost their child. It doesn't matter if it's the oldest, youngest or middle, but to lose my baby and just seen him and told him *I love you; don't get in no trouble,* [and he said] *I love you, too,* give me a hug and leave, and seven or eight hours down the road my baby's dead. It was like something just left my body. It wasn't [like] when you're sitting watching TV and you get a chill. It wasn't that. It was *I gave birth to this child. He came from me. That's part of my soul.* So half of my soul was gone; that's how I felt. It was a feeling I've never felt before. It's not like when he fell in the house, [or] he falls off his bike. It's not like the first time the police brought him home for trespassing. This was a feeling where part of my body; my soul was gone. I cannot describe it. People say, "Well Tasha, I'm so sorry to hear what you went through. I don't know how I would have got through it." Neither do I, [but] when I stop and think: God and [my son] LonEal get me through it. Because if I didn't have LonEal, I wouldn't have no reason to get up every day. My life was over.

[After the shooting, at the hospital] LonEal wanted to go in first. I asked [the nurse], I said, "Is he in a bag?" Because I did not want to see my son in no bag. She said, "No, he's not, Ms. Ross." LonEal said, "I'll go in first." I said, "I just don't want to see my son in no bag. If he's in a bag, will you please—" She said, "He's not in a bag; he's in that room down there." We went in this room. I opened it. I just screamed. I fell to my knees and LonEal grabbed me. Lamont was laying there like he was asleep but when I touched him there was nothing there. No feeling. No nothing. They had this blanket over him. I pulled it down. You could see a blood spot. They had this tube. I don't know what the tube was there for but it was this tube. It was just hanging there. I tried to clean him up but I couldn't. The blood wouldn't come off. That's when LonEal said, "Stop, Mama." Then LonEal covered him back up, and I prayed for him. I kissed him. And I let him go. There was nothing else I could do. I let him go. And I asked God why.

My first year was hell. I was alcoholic. I didn't care about nothing. I didn't take my blood pressure pills. One day my mom came. I was sitting up here in the dark, doors open, drinking, passed out on the couch. My mother got me up. She said, "You need to go to church." Went to church, sat down. All I could do was imagine my son's coffin here. I was sitting on this side but when we had services for him, I was sitting right up front, the second [or] third row. All I could imagine is my son's casket there. I got up, walked out of the church. My mom came outside, "Tasha, come back in." Why should I step in God's house when he let somebody take my child? I had no understanding. I didn't go to church again. My mom said, "You ain't going to never get this over with until you go to church." [Tasha did eventually go back to church, and was attending regularly at the time of the interview.]

But I was letting everything go. I just didn't care about nothin'. Sometimes I would get so drunk. I would be here by myself and I would pull out [Lamont's] sweaters and wrap them around me. The beginning, the first few months, you don't care about nothin'. You want to be mad at God because you don't understand why your child is not here. Why was that child taken? God didn't take my child. It took me three years to come to that. God did not take Lamont. He gave him everlasting life. So I appreciate that. He could have sent him to hell but he didn't do nothin' wrong to nobody. I'm at peace with it.

I'm angry, but I'm not mad at God no more. When you're having a bad day: *Oh, Jesus, get me through this.* That's who you call out. And if I can't say his name, whose am I going to say? I still don't understand why this happened, but I am not mad at God. I am not mad at Jesus. I'm not mad at the angels, disciples, or nobody. I'm mad at Edward Brown, Joshua Swan, and Candice [Edward's girlfriend]. Sister Marion told me I have to forgive them because God is going to forgive them. They are going to repent. My thing is, they're going to repent and God can forgive them all they want, but because I have so much anger in me, because I look at it like *Their parents are going to see them, they can talk to them*—I have to go to a gravesite.

March and June are really hard for me because Lamont's birthday is March 15. Usually I break down and cry and let it be *Why, why.* This year and last year was less. It was there but I wasn't angry. Maybe I came to accept that my son is gone, is not coming back. And I'm not going to see him until it's my turn.

So I still got a lot to do to get ready. But that's where I'm going to be. I'm going to be with him and it hurts. But I'm not mad at God no more. I'm mad at the people because God did not pull that trigger. My thing is, *You watch over everybody. You protect everybody. How can you let this man come and kill my son. Where was you at? Why did you let this happen?*

What triggers me? Say I'm at the mall or Wal-Mart and I see one of Lamont's friends. A lot of the kids come up to me. "Ain't you Lamont's mom?" I got kids telling me, "I was at Lamont's funeral, but you wasn't feeling too good." It makes me mad—not at them—but seeing them moving on with their lives . . . driving cars, working, having kids . . . I'm mad because they got a chance to move on and Lamont and DeMarco [friend killed at graduation party] and Felix didn't. That triggers it. That can ruin my whole day even though they are just saying hi and being polite. Just to see them move on. I don't know what's going on in their lives but just to see them two or three years older with their children or getting ready to get engaged; Lamont had that taken from him. It was taken from me. That triggers a lot of anger.

No one told me I was only going to have Lamont for seventeen years. If he came with instructions and on June 2 such and such is going to happen, then you prepare for it; you know this is going to happen on that day and you can't change it. But it didn't come like that. I thought I would get old and have grandkids and my sons would bury me. That's what I thought. That's everybody's thought, but that's not it. This is real, real life. This ain't no TV show where you turn on one week and somebody's lost in the woods for ten days with no water and food and a week later they found them and they're alive. This is not happening. My son is not walking through that door. Never again. I will never see Lamont Monroe until I make it to home. That's the last time I'm going to see him. That's just it.

I like looking over the TV and seeing a picture of my son. I sit there. I remember that day. I remember this day. Put it in God's hand. Take it one day at a time. Some days are better than others. There's nothing else to say. Some people say the pain goes away. The pain does not go away. Some days are better than others. I felt good getting up today. I know I passed my class. I know my son was there. I know I'm going to take my State exams on Saturday. But I feel good today. But a part of me knows Lamont's not going to be there with me. But he is right here in my heart. There's nothing else you can tell a person that loses their child. It's painful. It is so painful.

I'm not mad at God no more. I'm mad at the people because God did not pull that trigger.

My advice to others? Just tell them to go to church. Mothers who have recently lost their kids to gun violence—or parents who have lost their babies—you've got kids nineteen years old over in the war, not coming home. I pray for them, too. I pray that our soldiers come home. But I pray for those that don't make it home. The pain does not go away. For someone to sit there and tell you it does—I'd like to be drinking what they're drinking. That's not something you want to hear. Losing a brother, a sister, a mother, a father is hard, but to lose your child? There's articles that tell you you're not supposed to bury your children. Your children are supposed to bury you. I don't care if it's a car accident, shooting, airplane falling; you just don't want to lose your child.

I don't have closure. I never will have closure. I don't have closure. Just knowing they're [the killers] alive. I think, God forgive me, if they was to die tomorrow I might have closure. But I don't think that would give me closure because Lamont is not here. That's the key thing. The key thing is Lamont. He was trying to help someone and didn't know what he was doing. But thank God my son did not kill Edward Brown. I do. I don't know why. His mother would be going through what I'm feeling. I don't know what it would have done to my son. Some people kill people and flip out. God works in mysterious ways. Maybe he didn't want me to live knowing my son took somebody's life or not knowing if my son would be able to live if he took another person's life.

No regrets. None whatsoever. Because if I was to turn back the time, I probably wouldn't have gotten to know him. I don't think I would have had a good life, if that was the case. I am thankful to God that I got to know Lamont James Monroe, and I had him in my life for seventeen years. He was a blessing to me. I am grateful to God that I did have him for seventeen years. Because there's people that had kids—they died at birth, [or] four- and five-years-olds . . . I got to know him [Lamont] as a person. Yes, he did take me through a lot of things but if I had to redo time, I would not change nothing. I enjoyed every minute of Lamont James Monroe.

Tom Mauser May 2005

Tom's son, Daniel, along with twelve other students and a teacher at Columbine High School, was murdered on April 20, 1999, by two fellow students. Despite his anger and pain, he has become a national leader in the movement to outlaw automatic weapons and to keep guns out of the hands of criminals. He often speaks to large groups of people wearing the shoes Daniel was wearing the day he died.

I was at work and a coworker came in and started asking me a bunch of questions. He was very subtle. *Do you live in South Jeffco? Do you have a teenager?* and so on . . . I was getting ready to go to Pueblo for a conference. He said I should come into the meeting room to see what was going on on the TV. When I saw it I thought, *Oh, Columbine . . . Oh Daniel . . .* I didn't think about Daniel being involved. He was one of two thousand kids at Columbine but he was shy and would not be involved in any violence or something like that. I called my wife and she said she went to Leawood Elementary School where we were told to meet, along with all the other parents, but needed to be home when Daniel called.

One of my employees that I was going to Pueblo with said I needed to go home and he would go to Pueblo for me. I think he sensed that I was not acting right. Everything is really fuzzy because I don't remember a lot. Like I don't remember how I got to work that day or how I got home. It didn't really become serious for me until I heard the media say that a fourteen-year-old was

Tom Mauser

Tom's son Daniel

taken to one of the hospitals. Daniel was fourteen and that made it real for me—like it could be him.

I got to Leawood Elementary School and looked at the lists [of students who had safely arrived] but they were messy and confusing. There were lots of people there with lots of emotions. It was weird. Some people were happy because they were with their kids, and some were sad and worried because they hadn't seen theirs. I remember walking down the hall seeing Daniel's best friend coming towards me with his dad, thinking, *Why isn't Daniel with him?* I remember wanting to be like them, walking out with my son. I also felt a sense of, *Okay, let's get this over with, get Daniel and go home.*

There weren't any TVs or media in Leawood, so we really

did not know what was going on—we were just waiting. At one point they had all the parents who did not have their kids with them go into this other room. They said another bus is coming. So we waited but it was weird because Columbine and Leawood are pretty close together, maybe five minutes apart. I overheard someone say that they heard twenty people were dead. Forty-five minutes later I realized no bus was coming.

I said, "This is bullshit. No bus is coming," so I left. I started walking to my car, then I jogged, then I ran, and then I sprinted. I was crying. I finally got to my car and got out of the neighborhood. I was driving really fast and out of control. A policeman stopped me because I was going so fast. He asked, "What are you doing? What's going on?" I said, "My son, my son, I can't find my son . . . !" He said, "Enough people have died today, so why don't you slow down and be careful. Go home to your wife." We went to bed that night knowing that Daniel was dead. The next day his death was confirmed.

Right after Daniel's death I talked to a counselor that told me to be careful. That a lot of people who lose a child struggle with their marriage, and the divorce rate is really high. He also told me that people grieve in different ways. I am really glad I know that because it helped to know that. My wife is a very private person, and I am very public. Being public and talking about Daniel has helped me.

I hate it when people call it "the Columbine incident." When you trip, that is an incident. This was a massacre. A lot of people ask me, "How is the Columbine community?" I don't know how the community is. I am not a part of it. I am me and us. I think it is great, all the "We are Columbine" stuff, but I am not a part of that. When I hear someone on TV or on the news use the word *Columbine,* I don't think of me as being connected. I think

Tom putting on Daniel's shoes

of it as an event that happened that is not a part of me—like 9/11 was. My first thought is, *Oh yeah Columbine, how tragic.* My second thought is, *Oh yeah, that is Daniel; that is me. I am a part of that.* The other parents have been a great source of healing for me. I feel like they understand better than anyone. We all get together and it makes me feel better.

For the first anniversary we went to Glenwood Springs just to get through it. The media memorializes it, but you really just want it to be over. They memorialize the anniversary, but it's the birthdays, Mother's Day, Father's Day, and Christmas that are really hard. That is not what the media focus on. The most difficult one was Thanksgiving. It was really hard. Now it is a little easier, especially with our focus on Madeline [five-year-old daughter].

I don't get upset about the little things, and I feel compelled to tell people who do. I don't want to be rude, but when you go through losing a child it doesn't make sense to me for people to get so mad about the little things. I have always seen the sunny side of life. Until this I have had a great life—not tragedy. I felt really blessed. But now I think, *If this can happen to me then other stuff can happen.* I don't fear dying, because I know that I will be with Daniel, but I fear loss, the loss of my wife and daughters. I know what it feels like.

I felt like there have been signs from Daniel. Two days before Daniel's funeral, a vigil was held at St. Francis Cabrini Church for Daniel, Kelly Fleming, and Matt Kechter. Different people came up to eulogize the three victims. Unrehearsed. Christie [Daniel's older sister] spoke about the last time she saw Daniel on April 20. She told everyone how on that morning, as he left for school, Daniel told Christie he loved her. Christie said she knew Daniel loved her, but said that as a teen he never said it—except, of course, at a special time like Christmas.

The day of Daniel's funeral [April 25] was the same day a huge public memorial ceremony was held near Clement Park. The weather was cloudy and rainy. The funeral Mass was held at 5:15 that evening for Daniel and Kelly Fleming. When we entered the church, it wasn't raining but as the Mass began, the rain came. Near the end of the Mass, the two caskets were moved from one part of the church to another for the final prayers. Suddenly the rain stopped and the sun broke through a window that was way up high onto the two caskets.

The next day was also cloudy. I don't like April—not because of the anniversary but because of the weather. It reminds me of it all and how it was rainy and cold.

We drove twenty miles to Mt. Olivet Cemetery for Daniel's burial. As we drove along C-470 [a four-lane freeway on Denver's western edge] we noticed a herd of deer next to the road. It was an unusual time and location to see deer. They were a sign of comfort, and representative of Daniel's gentleness. Then as we drove to the cemetery, it was cloudy, with no sign of the sun. When we arrived at Mt. Olivet, the clouds parted and the sun shown down on us. It was so bright, I actually got hot. These were all signs.

On the second anniversary of the Columbine tragedy, Linda and I found ourselves traveling to Daniel's grave—something we don't do very much because of the painful memories. As we drove up C-470, I said to Linda that I had forgotten to look along the highway to see if there were any deer like on that day we buried Daniel. We were already near the end of C-470 but Linda said she had been watching, but didn't see any deer. Then as we were taking the ramp onto Interstate 70, we suddenly saw a large herd of deer next to the highway! There was just a thin sliver of open space, very close to a large housing subdivision. It was all very touching. We feel that God was telling us to not worry about Daniel.

I hate it when people call it "the Columbine incident." When you trip, that is an incident. This was a massacre.

Not a day goes by that I do not think about Daniel. I miss him a lot. I feel like we had a good life with him, and I feel really grateful that my wife was a stay-at-home mom. I used to give her a hard time because once the kids were in school, it seemed like she should go back to work. I am so glad now that she stayed at home. I have no regrets.

Loni Roberts May 2007

Loni and her husband Terry had been married for eighteen years when he went on a dream-of-a-lifetime hunting trip in Alaska with his long-time friend, Tim, and Tim's father, Gary. Due to a fatal hunting accident, he never came back. By the date of this interview, twelve years had passed. Loni and her sixteen-year-old son, Josh, adjusted to life without her husband and his father. Her identity as half of a couple died along with her husband, and she was left to figure out how to navigate life without her lifetime partner and friend.

Terry and Tim, one of his very best friends, planned this hunting trip for well over a year. Tim's father was going to go with them. It was a three-person hunting party. They had gone in a floatplane up the Bering River and had been dropped off. They were fishing for a week, and then they were going hunting for a week. Thursday night there was a bear that had come into their camp, and I guess it was a large bear. I don't know if it was a grizzly, brown, black, whatever. So a bear came into their camp, and they had to actually shoot at the bear to get it to leave. At that point, Tim's father, Gary was just incredibly spooked by the whole episode.

The next day they went out to go hunting. Terry and Tim were together and Gary went to another point where they were going to meet up. In order for Gary to get to that point, he had to cross over a creek and a swamp, and he had fallen into some water so

Loni Roberts

his gun had gotten wet. His scope had fogged up so this is where the stupidity starts just going crazy. He gets up there. He's still spooked about the bear situation at camp the night before. He was waiting for them, and he sees what he says he thought was an animal coming at him, three hundred yards away. At first, he said he thought it was a moose, but what he saw was their two faces and he thought it was the antlers of this moose. Then he thought it was a bear, and he couldn't see through his scope because his scope had fogged up. He shot anyway. Unfortunately, what he shot at was his son, whom he barely missed, and he shot my husband. He was not killed instantly; he actually bled to death.

They were hunting for moose and for bear. They had special permits. It was a dream trip that they had planned for well over a year. It's just very unfortunate. The part that probably makes it worse for me is that the following hunting season, Gary went hunting again, and I had a real problem with *Why is he still allowed to hunt?* I don't mind hunters as long as they follow the rules and everybody knows the safety features of everything; but to have killed somebody and then continue to hunt was a problem for me.

I did not speak to [Gary] after that. There was no way I could. He died of cancer several years after that. I still see Tim occasionally. He's always been very supportive. He felt a lot of guilt for a really long time. He probably still does. As I tried to explain to him, it's not his fault. He had no part in the accident. This was a trip that he and Terry had talked about, had dreamed of, had wanted to do for such a long time. There's no reason for him to feel guilty. It was his father who pulled the trigger.

I would say that my views on hunting have never changed because of this event. I still believe that it was stupidity that caused the event—not the hunting, not the guns. It was the fact that Gary failed to use reason and caution. Just because he'd been spooked by a bear in his camp and he still felt that anxiety or fear or whatever it was, he failed to follow the rules of hunting. If you can't see clearly, you don't shoot. It's not because he was hunting. It's not because he was using a gun. He failed as a human being.

Once you injure somebody, your right should be gone. That is the one thing that I think should change. Once you injure somebody because of [your] stupidity, [you] should lose that right. Unfortunately that didn't happen, and that part still bothers me. He continued to hunt after he had killed a human being. If he failed one time to follow common-sense rules for hunting, what's to stop him from doing it again? That's the only real issue I have with our rules of hunting.

I'm a realist. I always have been. There are things in life you can't change no matter what, and that's the way it is. I think a lot of that is a very deep faith. I happen to believe that God has a plan for all of us, and that's part of my plan. But what I had to work on is learning from it and not continuing to question. I could have questioned it for a very long time. It probably took me a couple years to get past that: *Why did this have to happen?* It happened, learn from it.

The only thing I may feel now is some depression. I think the anger is gone. I finally got past that. It was an act of stupidity. It wouldn't have changed if I'd been standing there. I have to accept that it happened and God has a plan for me that I don't know the result of, so I just have to deal with that aspect of it.

Terry and I met when we were seventeen and married when I was nineteen, so we kind of grew into adulthood together. We had a great relationship. I couldn't have seen an end to it, that's for sure. For the first month, September, and the first year [after he died], I would probably call it hibernation. I would just withdraw. Year two and year three you're trying to figure out . . . And this probably goes back to the fact that we were actually together since we were seventeen—at thirty-seven, you've been twenty years with one person. First, you grieve for your loss and then you try to figure out, *Okay, who am I? I've got to find out my identity as a human being on this planet without my partner.* Then at thirty-seven it's just like, *Whoa, I don't know who I am. I've always been part of a couple.* That was probably the hardest thing for me to get my brain around because you're always thinking, *Well, we . . . oh, it's not we, it's me.* We have to plan the weekend. Well we ain't planning the weekend. That was the difficult part for me personally—figuring out who I was. You are just one half of one couple. It was hard.

Because it's been twelve years, I can talk about it. When somebody asks me, "Are you married?" Well, I'm a widow. They stand back. Is it contagious? No! Trust me. They don't know what to say. For me to actually explain to them my husband was killed in a hunting accident—they clam up. It's easier for me to put them at ease. I learned that fairly early on because people I thought were friends, disappeared. Well you were friends before but now their phone doesn't work. I don't know, so that was a little hard to deal with. I don't think they knew how to deal with what to say. Most people don't know what to say. Instead of saying *I'm really sorry; I can't imagine what that would feel like*, it's just like, *No, you can't, trust me.* That's the thing people don't know how to deal with.

I think counseling really helped both me and my son, Josh. We could talk. We could allow ourselves to feel. It's just like,

Okay, I'm going to go into the other room now because I don't feel real good right now. Josh took grief counseling for about a year. He went through the adolescent grief counseling, and that truly helped us both. It's more focused on their needs, their reactions. It allows them to vent, get as angry as you want. They had a punching bag, areas where they could do art if they were artistic in some way. They were just able to get it out. The adult counseling is a little different because you tell your stories and you let yourself grieve that way. I've told everybody that's lost anyone since then, please go to grief counseling because we don't know how to deal with it. We're never taught how to deal with emotions like that. I don't care what your loss is from.

First, you grieve for your loss and then you try to figure out, *Okay, who am I? I've got to find out my identity as a human being on this planet without my partner. . . . I don't know who I am. I've always been part of a couple.*

Whether it's a loss from illness or auto accident or whatever, find counseling, find someone to be your support—find someone. I think that's the most important thing I can tell anybody else how to deal with this. Don't try to figure it out, because you can't. There is no answer. You can't find a definitive answer. It happened. It was hell. It truly was. It felt like you walked through the fires of hell and you kept waiting for the next block to drop on your head. Having that support system, knowing what the signs of grief were, knowing how to deal with it—that's what I tell everybody [because] I know what it's going to be, experiencing the loss of a loved one.

I am pretty happy with life in general because I accept the fact that there are no guarantees about it, and I enjoy every day as much as I can. We all have bad days. I love my house. I love my yard. I love to garden. I love sports. I love to go to baseball games. Those are the things I did before. Those are the things I do now. Those things haven't changed.

Tom Johnson (TJ)

His students called him "TJ." A hippie at heart, with a laid-back, friendly teaching style, he taught psychology at Columbine High School for over twenty years. Dylan Klebold and Eric Harris, the two students who shot and killed a teacher and twelve students at Columbine High School before killing themselves on April 20, 1999, were in his fifth-period class. Two weeks after the shooting, classes commenced at nearby Chatfield High School because so many repairs were needed at Columbine. TJ continued to teach at Columbine until the freshman who were there that horrible day graduated three years later.

We had a lunch routine; we never ate at school. We'd go to 7-Eleven, buy a scratch ticket, and drive back to school—me and Rick [Bath]. The first glint that I had that something was wrong [was as] we were driving back to the high school. Jeffco [Jefferson County] sheriff had the road blocked off, and we were forced to turn. We started winding our way through the community when we saw Brooks Brown either sitting on the sidewalk or sitting on the edge of the lawn. So I stopped the car. I said, "Brooks, what's going on?" He said, "Something bad is happening at the high school." From his body language I knew he was sincere. So at that point we pulled into the parking lot at Clement Park. I parked the car and got out, and there was a mass of people there. By just talking to people there, Rick and I found out that number one, there had been a shooting, and number two, it probably

156 • Beyond the Bullet

Tom Johnson

was Eric Harris and Dylan Klebold. I felt shocked. There was nothing in my experience or in my imagination where I could contemplate someone going into a school building and shooting kids.

I had faculty and staff that I couldn't find, our friends on the faculty that I couldn't find; I couldn't see them. I became very concerned about that. I didn't know which students had been either killed or injured, and I was concerned about that as well.

When something like this happens the first thing you do is take a look at your own mortality. You examine your behavior and your relationships. What I think a lot of people went through, and I think I'm probably the same way, is you almost become clingy around those that you love. You send a wife or kids to school, you expect them to come home.

The biggest mistake that I made, personally, was that the sheriff from Jeffco, one of his minions, said *If you have any information get it to us; here's the fax number.* When I got home, [I] printed out all my grade sheets, typed up about a four-page letter, and faxed it to them because that's what I thought I was supposed to do. Well two years later it ends up on a friggin' Web page—exactly what I sent them. That disturbed me because they never said this is going to become public information. I wish they would have, but they didn't.

I was in a dreamlike state from hypersensitivity. The day after the shooting—there was no school that day—I go to Safeway to buy some food and I'm in the produce section. When they are going to water the produce they start it off with thunder, and that just freaked me out. I was in a panic 'cause I thought it was happening there. I look at myself as being normal at the time, and I wasn't totally weirding out, but I was hypersensitive. Triggers for me are mostly calendar dates and outside events. You know, Virginia Tech . . . It all just brings it back.

TJ coaching at Columbine

There's also so much written about Columbine. The cast of players are always in the paper. I get tired of that, I really do. I just turn it off. At the beginning, I kept every single newspaper, I think, for about a week after the shooting, and then they started talking about [teacher] Judy Kelly and about me. They started talking about [teacher] Tom Tonelli, the counselors, the security officer. The actual Jeffco officer that was in the building fired a shot at them [at Harris and Klebold]. Then the comments about bullying came out, and the Trench Coat Mafia. At that point in time I said, *Well I think I've learned about as much as I need to know*. At that point I guess I started isolating myself.

My judgment has been clouded since 9/11 on a lot of things. I look at what those two did as a terrorist act, basically, and I think it's understandable for parents and media and members of the community to point fingers at the school. *You should have known this*. I never had a class in urban/suburban terrorist recognition in my life. I wouldn't know what to look for. Do I feel responsible for the shootings? Did I have any inclination they were coming? Absolutely not.

My perceptions have changed. I used to be a happy-go-lucky hippie—kind of a liberal, let the rough go with the smooth, bell-bottoms, Woodstock. I trusted people, and for the most part I liked people, and it didn't make any difference—male, female, black, white, orange, subterfuge, pinstriped. Now I'm not as trusting, and I don't like people as much. I find I'm easier to anger than I ever used to be, and it's not 'cause I'm old and crotchety. I find myself saying things, like when I'm driving, that I never would have said before. I've cursed before but the [current] frequency surprises me. I don't tolerate things the way I used to. I don't hold things. If someone cuts me off in traffic, yeah, I'll flip them off or say something. It happens in other places as well. When people are inconsiderate or rude, can't show a point of civility, don't show common courtesy, then I get angry but I don't carry the anger with me. I'm prone to anger [more easily]. It doesn't mean I'm stuck with this.

There was one point where I said, *I wish I could have met them [the shooters] in the parking lot with a handgun, and I would've shot both of them in the head*. The way it went down, I've got no choices at this point in time, where I was. I mean, this is something I'd done everyday—going off-campus for lunch. It would have been nice to have been there to offer support, because I couldn't get back into the building, obviously. I don't know. If I had been in the building, could I have done anything? Chances are, even though I thought I had a reasonable relationship with the two shooters, that had they seen me in the hallway they would have shot me dead. I have no idea of knowing. Why would they have let me go? What, 'cause I'm TJ? Buddy? Probably not. I regret that the event took place, and I'll go to my grave with that.

I never had a class in urban/suburban terrorist recognition in my life. I wouldn't know what to look for. Do I feel responsible for the shootings? Did I have any inclination they were coming? Absolutely not.

Yes, I have nightmares. In fact, I had one last night. It's about the shooting. Sometimes I end up with a tag on my toe. Just a feeling of helplessness, I think. Being out of control in the situation. But they are fewer. Usually they are timed to calendar dates. As we get closer to [April 20], I'll start having dreams again. Something pops up on the news or in the newspaper that I happen to catch—it will happen then.

I saw a therapist for a while. I met with him for maybe six or eight weeks, one hour a week. My Kaiser physician gave me some Xanax which chilled me right out 'cause I was having anxiety attacks, especially when I was driving to Chatfield [High School where Columbine was temporarily relocated to after the shooting] to teach. I said, "I can't do this." Teaching at Chatfield was the worst experience. The whole thing was weird. The first day . . . I said I don't know what I'm going to tell these kids come that fifth-hour class where the two shooters were. It went as well as to be expected, the people that were there . . . I just switched things out. We stopped psychology [coursework] and worked on collages and watched Adam Sandler movies just to get through. We weren't given any instruction on what to do. We pretty much just had to figure it out. At that point I had twenty-two or twenty-three years teaching experience, and I don't know what they could have told me to do. I mean, I don't know. I just went with the flow. It went okay. They got through; they went through graduation. Two of my students were killed—Harris and Klebold—but I knew many of the other students killed.

Many of my students wrote essays about it, but as close as it was, I didn't know what to say to them. I don't think it was a good idea to return to school, but it was good for the kids to have some closure on their school year. But what a painful, painful three weeks that was. We were there from one to six in the afternoon. You've got teachers crying all over the place.

I [remember waking] up on April 21st at 3:00 a.m., and I said, "Oh my god, my coffee pot and my computer in my classroom are still on!" And it hit me like a bolt out of the blue. "Oh my god, they're still on!" So at three in the morning I called Jeffco sheriff 'cause I'm afraid of a fire and I said, "Ma'am, you're not going to believe this . . . my name is Tom Johnson, I teach at Columbine, room SS-5." I said, "I think we may have an issue here, 'cause I left my computer and coffee pot on." And I said, "I don't want a fire." She said, "Sir, we'll take care of that, okay?" So I go back in mid-June and [they were] still on; the coffee pot and computer. I was not a happy camper about that, but who are you going to call? The coffee pot still worked; the computer was fried. [In retrospect, TJ recognized the absurdity of worrying about a coffee pot when so much of the building had already been destroyed—an example of the "hypersensitivity" he talked about earlier in the interview.]

I taught until the freshman who were there graduated, 2003. People were scared to discipline the kids and to some extent it is still the same way even though the only connection that most of the kids from Columbine have with that event would be older brothers and sisters. You need to kind of pull the kids back in, but everyone was walking on eggshells. There were kids that would play "the Columbine card" at any opportunity. Staff members, too. I can understand that, but you can't let them go that far and then expect to pull them back in and have them focus on what they need to do. Discipline was a disaster.

The lawsuits? I can't remember if there were seven, eight, or nine. It doesn't make any difference 'cause there were a bunch of us that were sued. Their point [the claimants'] was that there were enough red flags that a reasonable, prudent person would have picked up on that. In my case it was [an assignment on a] dream interpretation, a thing we did about six weeks prior to the shooting. That really hurt me. Had I known that this was coming, I would have done something about it. That bothered me a great deal. You always second-guess. Should I have done something? I went over that and over that again, and sometimes I say, *Maybe I should have seen something* and sometimes I say, *What could I have seen?* I'm not a mind reader. We also live in a litigious society.

Education will not be the same after April 20, 1999. We had no protocols back then because it was so unimaginable that someone would be in the building armed. Now they have inside drills, they have outside drills, not just fire drills, evacuation drills . . . At least now they have protocols for that. They sure didn't back then.

Tom Johnson (TJ) • 163

My journey

When I started interviewing people for this book I thought I would be *taking* from each person. I worried that I was asking too much of the interviewees, or that my involvement would be seen as somehow voyeuristic. I was surprised at how willing each person was to talk to me. I was also surprised at how grateful they were for my willingness to listen to them.

I asked Michelle (pg 82) if she had talked to someone like a counselor or minister about the anguish she felt. She simply replied, "I've talked to God and I've talked to you." When I was talking to Sandie (pg 108) I paused the interview because she seemed to be sobbing uncontrollably. I told her I didn't want to re-traumatize her; that we could stop now. She immediately stopped crying and said, "This is great," that she had never had the opportunity to tell her story uninterrupted. And then she thanked me, continued crying, and continued telling her story. As we drove away, Kathy, the photographer, and I both got the distinct feeling that she did not want us to go.

I found that after each interview I walked out the door bearing a heavy load. I was honored to be trusted with each person's devastation, pain, and vulnerability, but I was aware that I needed to protect myself from being traumatized by their stories. After one especially long and emotionally intense interview in Colorado, Kathy and I got into the car and drove onto the highway. About a half-mile later I said, "I can't do this." I pulled over at the next exit and we just sobbed. For twenty minutes we continued to cry in silence knowing that we had shared an incredibly intimate moment. Taking time immediately to release such intense emotions became an important, and private, part of the process for us in subsequent interviews.

I'm so grateful for the opportunity to be a part of the lives of the people in this book, if only for a small amount of time.

Heidi Yewman

Gun violence in perspective

The people in this book represent a very small fraction of people impacted by gun violence. Every year, approximately thirty thousand people are killed by guns in the United States. Over seventy thousand are injured. The following pages illustrate just how gun violence impacts our country.

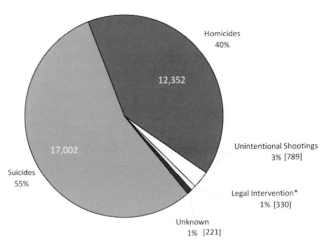

Gun Deaths, United States, 2005

Homicides
40%

12,352

17,002

Suicides
55%

Unintentional Shootings
3% [789]

Legal Intervention*
1% [330]

Unknown
1% [221]

Source: Brady Center to Prevent Gun Violence, based on data from the WISQARS system, www.cdc.gov/ncipc/wisqars/, accessed 9-30-2008.

*Legal Intervention: "Injuries inflicted by the police or other law-enforcing agents . . . in the course of arresting or attempting to arrest lawbreakers, suppressing disturbances, maintaining order, and other legal action."

Non-Fatal Gun Injuries, United States, 2005

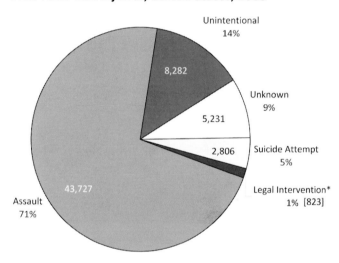

Source: Brady Center to Prevent Gun Violence, based on data from the NEISS system, www.cdc.gov/ncipc/ 10-01-2008.

*Legal Intervention: "Injuries inflicted by the police or other law-enforcing agents . . . in the course of arresting or attempting to arrest lawbreakers, suppressing disturbances, maintaining order, and other legal action."

Gun Deaths and Non-Fatal Gun Injuries, United States, 2005

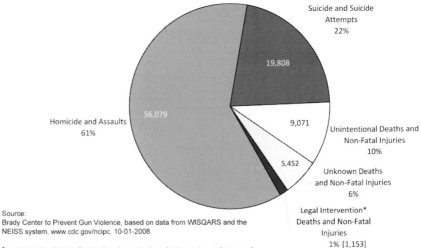

Suicide and Suicide Attempts
22%

19,808

Homicide and Assaults
61%

56,079

9,071

Unintentional Deaths and Non-Fatal Injuries
10%

5,452

Unknown Deaths and Non-Fatal Injuries
6%

Legal Intervention*
Deaths and Non-Fatal Injuries
1% [1,153]

Source:
Brady Center to Prevent Gun Violence, based on data from WISQARS and the NEISS system, www.cdc.gov/ncipc, 10-01-2008.

*Legal Intervention: "Injuries inflicted by the police or other law-enforcing agents . . . in the course of arresting or attempting to arrest lawbreakers, suppressing disturbances, maintaining order, and other legal action."

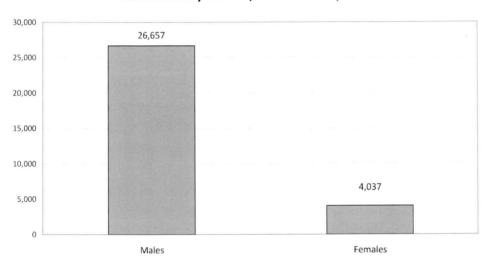

Gun Deaths by Gender, United States, 2005

Males: 26,657
Females: 4,037

Source:
Brady Center to Prevent Gun Violence, based on data from the WISQARS
system, www.cdc.gov/ncipc/wisqars/, accessed 9-30-2008.

Gun Deaths by Race/Ethnicity, United States, 2005

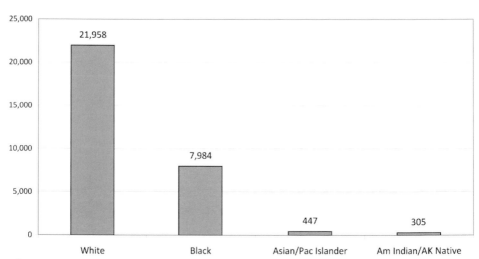

Source:
Brady Center to Prevent Gun Violence, based on data from the WISQARS system,
www.cdc.gov/ncipc/wisqars/, accessed 9-30-2008.

Gun Deaths by Age Group, United States, 2005

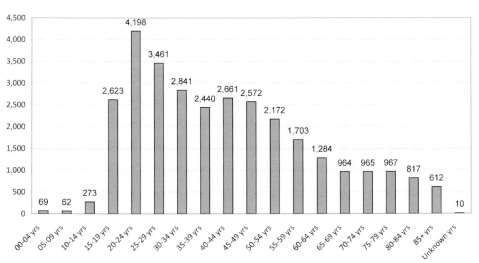

Source:
Brady Center to Prevent Gun Violence, based on data from the WISQARS
system, www.cdc.gov/ncipc/wisqars/, accessed 9-30-2008.

Resources/Organizations for Victims

The following list of national resource organizations provides resources, literature, and Web site links to many other national, state, and local victims' organizations.

Office for Victims of Crime (OVC)
800-627-6872
www.ojp.usdoj.gov/ovc

National Center for Victims of Crime (NCVC)
800-394-2255
www.ncvc.org

National Organization for Victim Assistance (NOVA)
800-879-6682
www.trynova.org

Parents of Murdered Children (a self-help group dedicated to helping the families and friends of those who have lost their lives to violence)
888-818-7662
www.pomc.com

Bereaved Parents of the USA (a nationwide organization dedicated to helping bereaved parents and families)
708-748-7866
www.bereavedparentsusa.org

Murder Victims Families of Human Rights (works *for* victims and *against* the death penalty)
617-491-9600
www.murdervictimsfamilies.org

Witness Justice (a national nonprofit organization offering direct services for survivors of violence and their allies who are experiencing difficulties)
800-495-4357
www.witnessjustice.org

American Society of Suicidology (promotes a better understanding of suicidal people and suicide prevention)
202-237-2280
www.suicidology.org

Concern of Police Survivors (COPS) (provides resources to assist in rebuilding the lives of surviving families of law enforcement officers killed in the line of duty)
573-346-4911
www.nationalcops.org

Attorney General's Financial Assistance (provides services—including financial assistance—to crime victims and witnesses whose cases are prosecuted by the Office of the Attorney General in each state)
*Contact your local Attorney General's office

National Crime Prevention Council (nonprofit educational group formed to address the causes of crime and violence and to reduce the opportunities for crime to occur)
202-466-6272
www.ncpc.org

Gunvictims.org (Brady Center to Prevent Gun Violence: tribute and memorial page for those who have lost a loved one to gun violence)
202-898-0792
www.bradycenter.org/victims

Vinelink (an online service that allows crime victims to obtain timely and reliable information about criminal cases and the custody status of offenders twenty-four hours a day)
*Each state has its own VINE Service number. Check the Web site to get the number for your state.
www.vinelink.com

About the photographer

I grew up in Alaska, hunting, fishing, and fully embedded in a culture of guns and gun ownership. I never thought about the effect guns can have until I met Heidi Yewman. Before we embarked on this project, she had come over to my house for a visit. She asked what should have been an easy question, "Do you have a gun in the house?" Yes, I did have a gun in my house and that was the easy part of the question. "Is it locked up?" This wasn't as easy for me to answer.

On our first assignment, just a short drive to Lonnie Feather's house in Southeast Portland, Oregon, my eyes started to open to the real impact of guns. Lonnie was shot three times by her boyfriend, who first put a pillow over her face. She then pretended to be dead for seven hours before being able to secretly dial 911. I took the photos as Lonnie pointed to the places in her house where this horror had happened, and told Heidi about her "star nebula"—the scar on her cheek that she refuses to fix, as a reminder. Aside from the evening news, I had never heard such words come out of anyone's mouth.

I was astonished. Could you live in the same house where something like that happened to you? On the drive home I thought about Lonnie and about my three small children—and the gun sitting in my house, unlocked and loaded. And why had I felt like I had to lie when I told Heidi that the gun was locked up?

Over the next several months, Heidi and I heard and recorded heartbreaking stories. Kids accidentally shooting friends. Suicides. Tragedies—all involving guns. I began to question why I had a gun in my house. Was it really about protection? Was it the Alaskan in me? But the mother in me couldn't forget the eyes of the people whose father, mother, brother, sister, or child had died. I didn't want that kind of pain.

I am inspired by these stories, by the ability of people to continue living in the face of awful tragedies. I've learned how the daily reality of pain and loss looks—up close and personal. It made me realize that removing the gun from my house made it less likely that I would live through one of their realities. I am fortunate to have met every person in this book. I have been touched by their strength, courage, and their ability to make a difference. They have all made a difference in my life by opening my eyes. My hope is that my photographs will portray the strength of those who live on, despite the daily anguish.

I grew up in Alaska where guns were—and still are—a part of everyday life. But after being so close to so much pain, I simply cannot be as close to the gun culture. Thinking back, I can remember people in Alaska who were killed or injured by guns. But at the time, my eyes weren't open to those stories, that possibility.

They are now.

Kathy Carlisle